ARCHITECTURAL RENDERING
TECHNIQUES /A COLOR REFERENCE

ARCHITECTURAL RENDERING
TECHNIQUES /A COLOR REFERENCE

MIKE W. LIN, ASLA

VNR VAN NOSTRAND REINHOLD COMPANY
New York

Every effort has been made to give proper credit to individuals whose work is included in this book. Any corrections brought to the attention of the publisher will be incorporated into future printings.

Illustrations copyright © 1985 by Mike W. Lin
Library of Congress Catalog Card Number 84-25812
ISBN 0-442-25953-0

Printed in Hong Kong
Designed by Mike W. Lin and Bacci Design

Published by Van Nostrand Reinhold Company Inc.
135 West 50th Street
New York, New York 10020

Van Nostrand Reinhold Company Limited
Molly Millars Lane
Wokingham, Berkshire RG11 2PY, England

Van Nostrand Reinhold
480 La Trobe Street
Melbourne, Victoria 3000, Australia

Macmillan of Canada
Division of Canada Publishing Corporation
164 Commander Boulevard
Agincourt, Ontario M1S 3C7, Canada

16 15 14 13 12 11 10 9 8 7 6 5 4 3 2 1

Library of Congress Cataloging in Publication Data
Lin, Mike W.
   Architectural rendering techniques.

   Bibliography: p.
   1. Architectural rendering—Technique.   I. Title.
NA2780.L56   1985   720'.28'4   84-25812
ISBN 0-442-25953-0

Contents

To JoAnn with love

Preface

Are you interested in clearly expressing your ideas and concepts through graphic communication? It is my intention for people to trace, imitate, and use this portfolio to build confidence in their drawing ability and to develop ideas. Students and professionals in architecture, interior design, landscape architecture, and graphic design, and illustrators from all disciplines, can use this book to save time and improve graphic and architectural rendering techniques. I believe that everyone is capable of producing high-quality graphics. The keys to successful drawing include a willingness to try, a willingness to make mistakes and accept criticism, and a willingness to practice until the mistakes are corrected.

This color portfolio consists of examples that could be used as a learning file and/or reference book. The arrangement and organization of this book follow a progression from simple line drawings to detailed final presentations, and from loose sketches to tight illustrations. It is divided into sections of media comparison; entourage and details; site analyses, plans, elevations, and sections; loose sketches; and exterior and interior illustrations.

These drawings are arranged in the following order: pencil, ink, color pencil, pastel, marker, acrylic, watercolor, tempera, and airbrush. The illustrations are also in sequence from small to large scale. Every drawing is identified, when possible, with the artist's name and location, the medium, the size and type of paper, and the time required to execute the drawing. Some drawings end with the symbol (T). This indicates that the artist traced the original artwork; initial blockout time for that drawing is not included. Credits for the designer and/or company are in the Appendix.

The examples in this color portfolio cover many subjects as well as different techniques and approaches to various graphic methods. These enable the viewer to choose according to the style preferences and needs of a client. This prototype is a compilation of professionals' work, my own work, and the work of present and past students and participants at universities and workshops across the nation. This demonstrates that any student, professional, or interested person can succeed with proper guidance and examples. The goal is to increase one's ability to draw quickly and comfortably, and most important, to excel in graphic and rendering techniques.

Acknowledgments

This color portfolio of architectural rendering techniques was made possible by the efforts of many individuals and groups whose assistance is greatly appreciated. Thanks are extended to the Kansas State University faculty for their academic support, especially to Professor Thomas Musiak. The American Society of Landscape Architects and many of its local chapters have sponsored numerous national and local tours enabling me to travel, stay in touch, and gain ideas from various professionals. Special gratitude is given to the students and professionals across the country who attended my graphic workshops at various locations or at Kansas State University. They made me aware of the need for this portfolio.

Very special thanks are due to the many individuals who contributed work that appears in this book. Many students at Kansas State University, too many to mention, have helped to compile this information. Their efforts have proven to be invaluable. Also, thanks go to Wendy Lochner at Van Nostrand Reinhold for her patience and assistance.

Special gratitude is extended to my wife, JoAnn, for her understanding, patience, encouragement, and support; and to my son, Brian, and daughter, Sharon.

MEDIA COMPARISON

1

Leslie Carow, student, Colorado State University. Felt-tip pen and black marker on individual 9"-x-12" bond paper. 20 minutes to 1½ hours each. (T)

Leslie Carow, student, Colorado State University. Watercolor on 8"-x-12" watercolor paper. 1 hour. (T)

Leslie Carow, student, Colorado State University. Marker, felt-tip pen, and airbrush on 8"-x-12" bond paper. 1 hour. (T)

Leslie Carow, student, Colorado State University. Marker, airbrush, and colored pencil on 8"-x-12" marker paper. 1 hour. (T)

Dick Sneary, illustrator, Kansas City, MO. Black colored pencil and pastel on 19"-x-24" yellow tracing paper. 1 hour. (T)

Dick Sneary, illustrator, Kansas City, MO. Sharpie pen on 19"-x-24" printed brown-line diazo print paper. 1 hour. (T)

Michael Flynn, student, Kansas State University. No. 2 pencil on 19"-x-24" vellum. 5 hours. (T)

Mike W. Lin. Felt-tip pen on 19"-x-24" vellum. 2 hours.

Paul Adams, landscape architect, Florida. Marker and felt-tip pen on 19"-x-24" marker paper. 2½ hours. (T)

Kevin Kerwin, student, Kansas State University. Marker, airbrush, and tempera on 19"-x-24" marker paper. 5 hours. (T)

Robert Holzwarth, student, Kansas State University. Marker, airbrush, and white colored pencil on 19"-x-24" brown sepia. 4 hours. (T)

Kathryn Marsh, student, Kansas State University. Paper collage (magazine fragments) on 19"-x-24" paper. 16 hours. (T)

Mike W. Lin. Marker, tempera, pastel, and colored pencil on 19"-x-24" marker paper. 14 hours.

Paul Muus, student, North Dakota State University. Marker and airbrush on 19"-x-24" marker paper. 1½ hours. (T)

Left: Joan Minnemau, student, Kansas State University. Nos. 00 and 000 ink pen on 9½"-x-12" vellum. 5 hours. (T) *Right*: Danny Potts, student, Kansas State University. Nos. 00 and 000 ink pen on 9½"-x-12" vellum. 7 hours. (T)

Kathryn Marsh, student, Kansas State University. Felt-tip pen with colored Pantone paper and black-and-white Zipatone on 9½"-x-12" paper. 40 minutes each. (T)

Student, Kansas State University. Felt-tip pen on 8½"-x-11" paper towel. 20 minutes. (T)

George Holton, student, Kansas State University. No. 00 ink pen on 8½"-x-11" vellum. 3 hours. (T)

Donald Rakoski, student, Kansas State University. Brown felt-tip pen and marker on 8½-x-11" diazo print paper. 3½ hours. (T)

Robert Holzwarth, student, Kansas State University. Marker and felt-tip pen on 7½"-x-9" rice paper. 1 hour. (T)

Douglas Saulsbury, student, Kansas State University. Black colored pencil on 7½"-x-9" vellum. 7 hours. (T)

Douglas Saulsbury, student, Kansas State University. Colored pencil on 7½"-x-9" watercolor paper. 9 hours. (T)

James Bohn, student, Kansas State University. No. 1 ink pen on 7½"-x-9" vellum. 4 hours. (T)

Danny Potts, student, Kansas State University. No. 000 ink pen on 7½"-x-9" vellum. 8 hours. (T)

Danny Potts, student, Kansas State University. Pencil on 7½"-x-9" vellum. 3 hours. (T)

Brian Fisher, student, Kansas State University. Tempera and watercolor on 7½"-x-9" watercolor paper. 4 hours. (T)

Ted Morningstar, architect, Chicago, IL. Hand-drawn on T.V. monitor using Mindset computer and
printed on 6"-x-8" computer paper with Diablo C150 inkjet printer. 4 hours.

Lucy Hu, student, Louisiana State University. Paper collage (magazine fragments) on 8½"-x-11" paper. 10 hours. (T)

ENTOURAGE
AND DETAILS

2

Marjorie Pitz, landscape architect, Minneapolis, MN. Pencil and felt-tip pen on 12"-x-24" yellow tracing paper and vellum, respectively. 1½ hours each.

Participants, Kansas State University graphic workshop. Felt-tip pen, pastel, and marker on various sizes and types of paper. 2 minutes to ½ hour each.

Lower left: Steve Beyer, student, University of Minnesota. Pencil and colored pencil on 6"-x-10" yellow tracing paper. ½ hour. *Top and right:* Dick Sneary, illustrator, Kansas City, MO. Felt-tip pen and colored pencil on 12"-x-14" bond paper. 10 seconds to 10 minutes each.

Brian Maugh, student, Kansas State University; Dick Sneary, illustrator, Kansas City, MO. Felt-tip pen, colored pencil, and pastel on 19"-x-24" bond paper. 5 minutes to 30 minutes each.

Michael E. Doyle, illustrator, Boulder, CO. Marker and colored pencil on 3"-x-8" (left) and 9"-x-12" (right) bond paper. 30 minutes (left), 3 hours (right).

Left: Ken Swihart, student, Kansas State University. Marker, pastel, and colored pencil on 8"-x-14" bond paper. 3 hours. (T) *Right:* Brian Rothman, student, Kansas State University. Pastel on 12"-x-18" pastel paper. 2 hours.

San-Chin Kao, architect, Taiwan. Watercolor on 12"-x-16" pastel paper. 1 hour.

Participants, Kansas State University graphic workshop. Marker on 14"-x-16" marker paper. 10 minutes each.

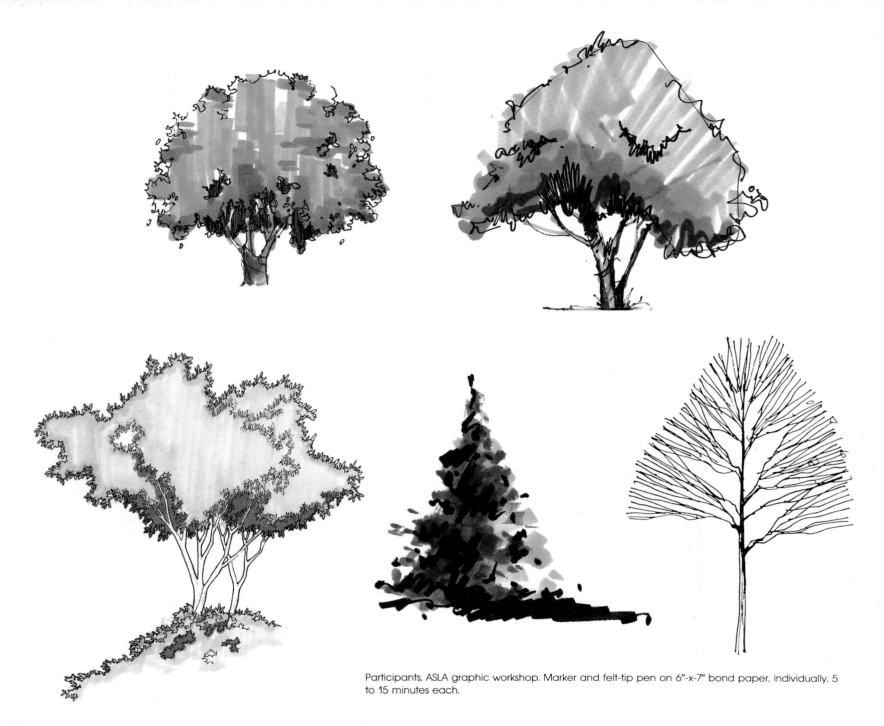

Participants, ASLA graphic workshop. Marker and felt-tip pen on 6"-x-7" bond paper, individually. 5 to 15 minutes each.

46

Wayne Williams, professor, Washington State University. Watercolor, colored pencil, pastel, and felt-tip pen on 8"-x-10" paper, individually. 20 minutes each.

Left: Wayne Williams, professor, Washington State University. Marker on 10"-x-10" rice paper. 45 minutes. *Right:* Dick Sneary, illustrator, Kansas City, MO. Marker on 17"-x-22" bond paper. 15 minutes.

white space

Participants, ASLA graphic workshop. Pencil, Sharpie pen, and marker on individual 8"-x-10" bond paper. 5 to 20 minutes each.

Thomas Wang, professor, University of Michigan. Marker on 8"-x-10" bond paper. 40 minutes.

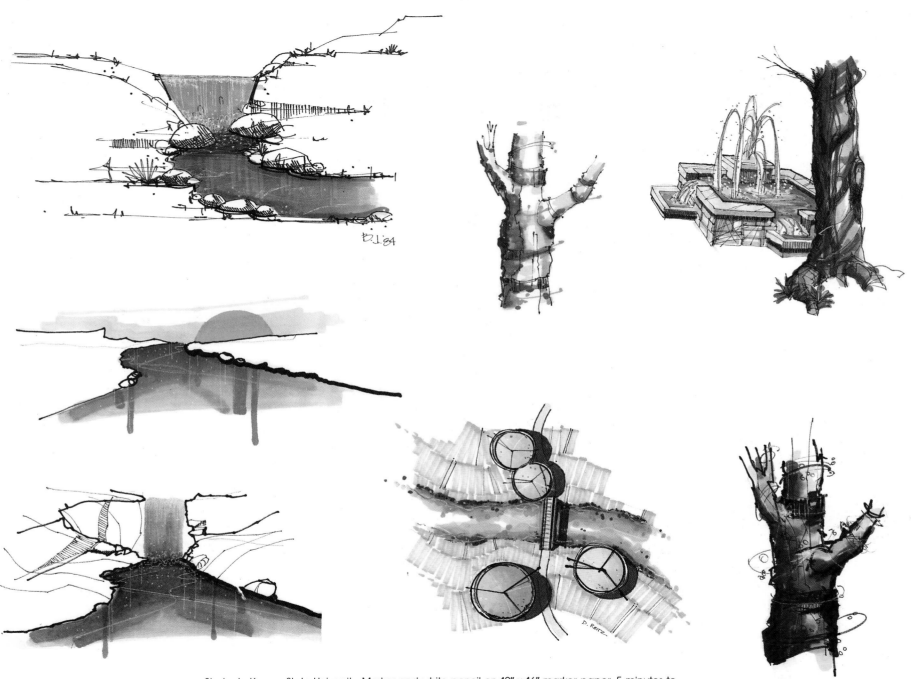

Students, Kansas State University. Marker and white pencil on 10"-x-16" marker paper. 5 minutes to ½ hour each.

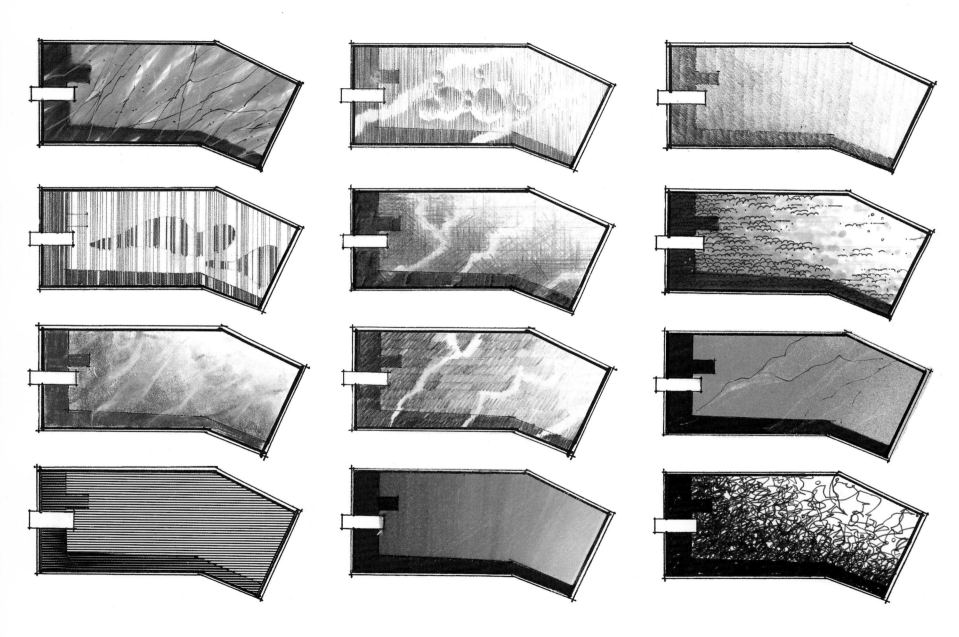

Students, Kansas State University. Various techniques on different 2"-x-5" papers. 5 to 15 minutes each. (T)

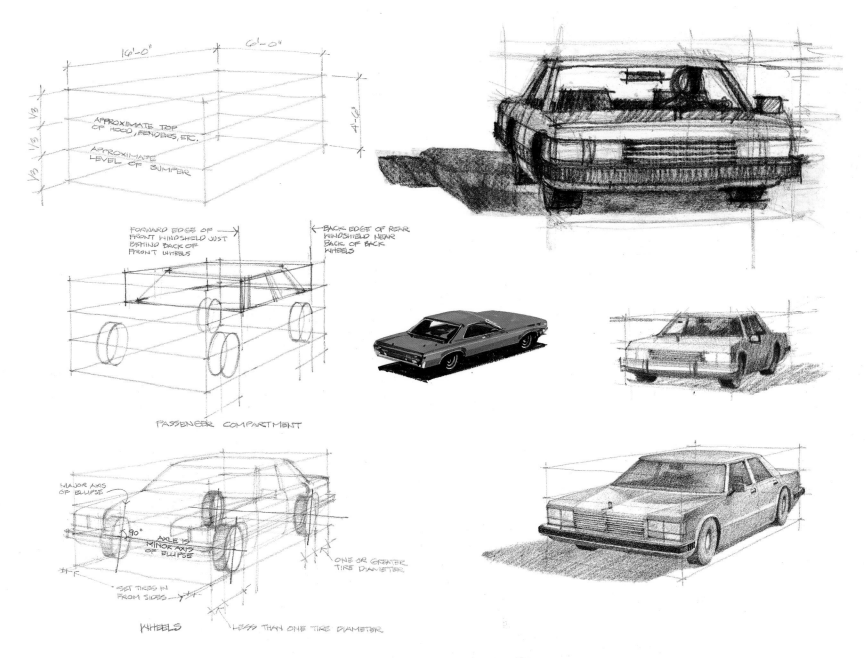

16'-0" 6'-0"

⅓ ⅓ ⅓   4'-6"

APPROXIMATE TOP
OF HOOD, FENDERS, ETC.

APPROXIMATE
LEVEL OF BUMPER

FORWARD EDGE OF
FRONT WINDSHIELD JUST
BEHIND BACK OF
FRONT WHEELS

BACK EDGE OF REAR
WINDSHIELD NEAR
BACK OF BACK
WHEELS

PASSENGER COMPARTMENT

MAJOR AXIS
OF ELLIPSE

90°
AXLE IS
MINOR AXIS
OF ELLIPSE

ONE OR GREATER
TIRE DIAMETER

SET TIRES IN
FROM SIDES

WHEELS   LESS THAN ONE TIRE DIAMETER

Dick Sneary, illustrator, Kansas City, MO. Colored pencil and tempera on 19"-x-25" marker paper. 10 minutes to 40 minutes each.

Top left: Mike W. Lin. Marker on 5"-x-8" marker paper.
20 minutes. *Top right:* Sheryl Brolander, student, Iowa
State University. Marker on 8"-x-10" rice paper. 40 minutes.
Bottom: Student, Rhode Island School of Design. Airbrush,
pencil, and white tempera on 5"-x-14"
bond paper. 30 minutes.

Top: Nancy Ewalt, instructor, Texas Tech University. Marker, colored pencil, and white tempera on 6"-x-18" marker paper. 8 hours. (T) *Bottom:* Sheryl Brolander, student, Iowa State University. Marker, colored pencil, and white tempera on 6"-x-14" marker paper. 8 hours. (T)

Left: Douglas Hahn, student, Kansas State University. Marker, white colored pencil, and tempera on 5"-x-6" marker paper. 3 hours. (T) *Right:* Marc Silva, student, Kansas State University. Marker, white colored pencil, and tempera on 7"-x-9" marker paper. 5 hours. (T)

Barbara Hoffman, student, Kansas State University. Marker and white tempera on 14"-x-18" marker paper. 30 minutes each.

Left: H.W.I., student, Kansas State University. Marker and tempera on trimmed 5"-x-8" bond paper, pasted over brown construction paper. 1 hour. (T) *Right:* Rita Eddy, student, Kansas State University. Colored pencil on 6"-x-8" yellow tracing paper. 1 hour. (T)

Left: Kathleen Heimerman, student, Kansas State University. Marker and white tempera on trimmed 8"-x-11" marker paper, pasted over black construction paper. 2 hours. (T) *Right:* Mark Flamm, student, Kansas State University. Marker and colored pencil on trimmed 8"-x-11" marker paper, pasted over mat-board with airbrush background. 2 hours. (T)

Participants, Kansas State University graphic workshop. Marker and colored pencil on 19"-x-24" marker paper. 10 to 40 minutes each.

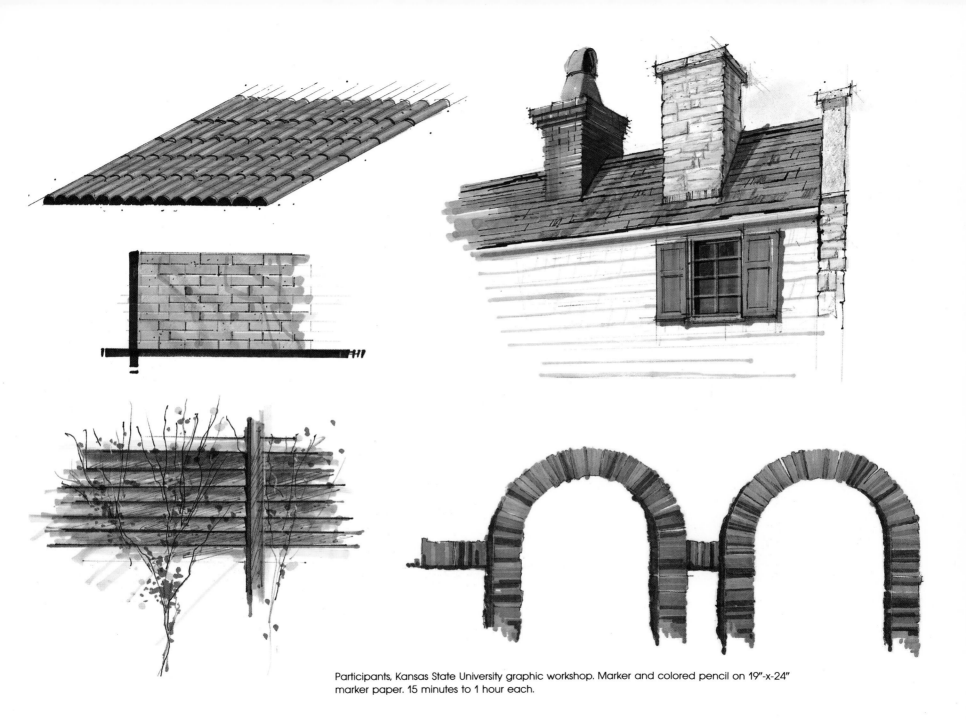

Participants, Kansas State University graphic workshop. Marker and colored pencil on 19"-x-24" marker paper. 15 minutes to 1 hour each.

Professional illustrator, Kansas City, MO. Tempera on 10"-x-18" Crescent 100 board. 15 to 40 minutes each.

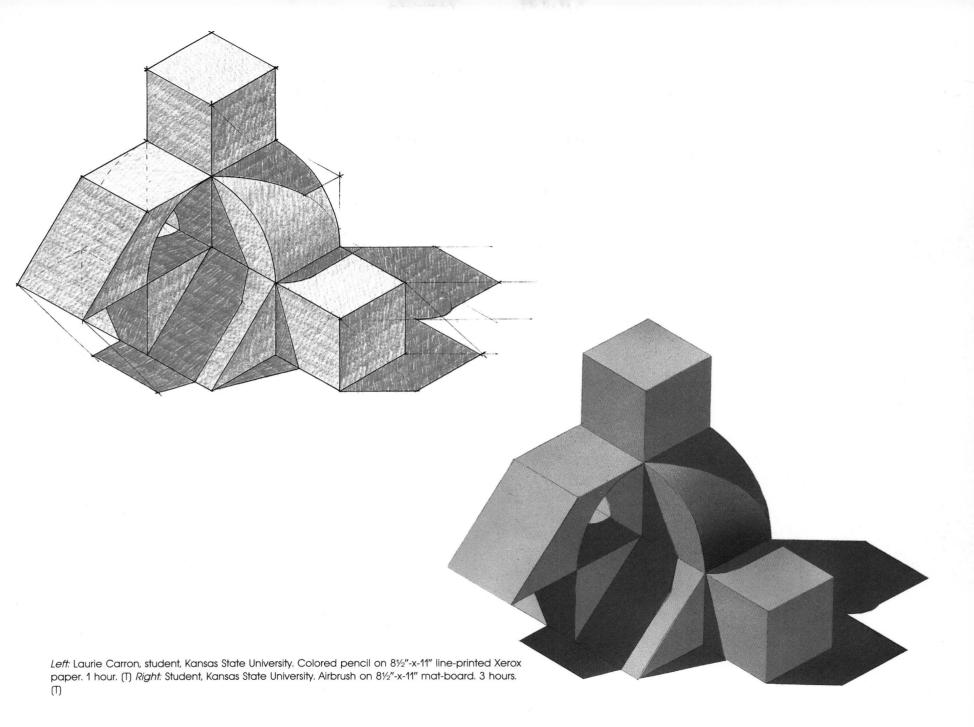

Left: Laurie Carron, student, Kansas State University. Colored pencil on 8½"-x-11" line-printed Xerox paper. 1 hour. (T) *Right*: Student, Kansas State University. Airbrush on 8½"-x-11" mat-board. 3 hours. (T)

63

Top: Anne Hunt, student, England. Pencil, colored pencil, felt-tip pen, and pastel on 12"-x-18" bond paper. 1½ hours. *Lower left:* Laurie Carron, student, Kansas State University. *Lower right:* Edward Stewart, landscape architect, Sarasota, FL. Marker and colored pencil on individual 8"-x-10" marker paper. 2 hours (left), 1 hour (right).

Participants, Kansas State University graphic workshop. Marker, felt-tip pen, and colored pencil on 19"-x-24" marker paper. 2 hours.

Top: Paul Haberman, architect, Dallas, TX. *Bottom:* Larry Taylor, student, Kansas State University. Both F pencil on 8½"-x-11" vellum. 15 minutes each.

SITE ANALYSES/
PLANS/
ELEVATIONS/
SECTIONS

3

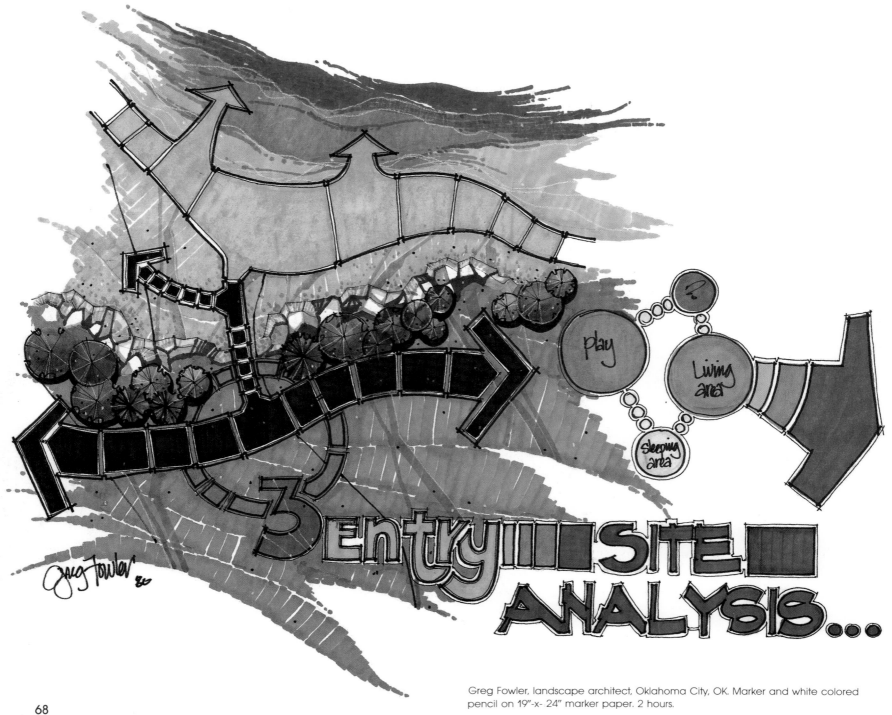

3 Entry Site Analysis...

play

Living area

sleeping area

Greg Fowler, landscape architect, Oklahoma City, OK. Marker and white colored pencil on 19"-x-24" marker paper. 2 hours.

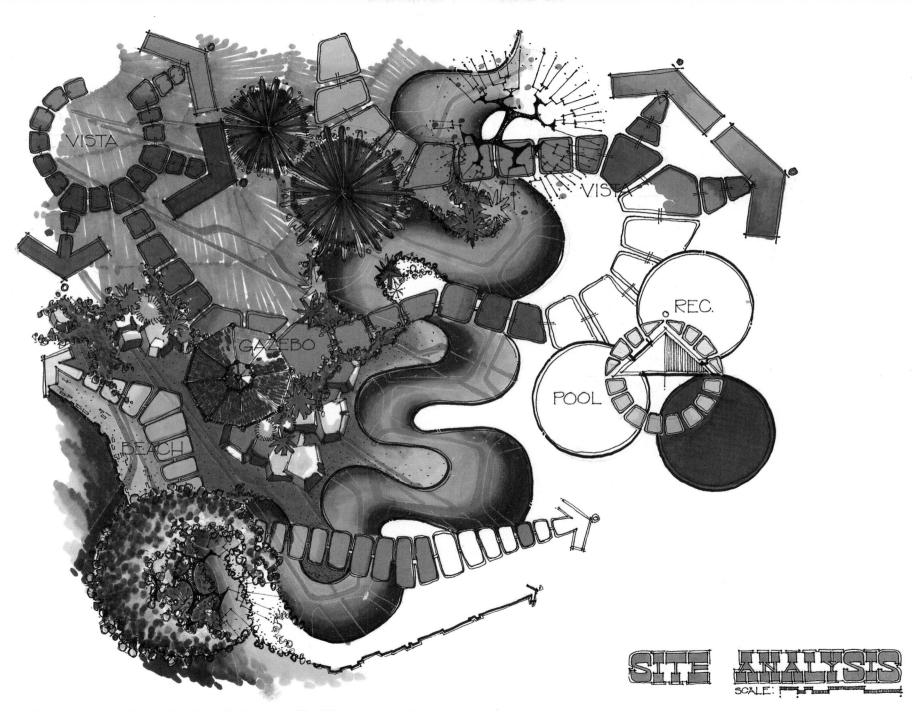

VISTA

VIST

REC.

GAZEBO

POOL

BEACH

SITE ANALYSIS

SCALE:

Kevin Karst, student, Kansas State University. Marker on 19"-x-24" marker paper. 5 hours.

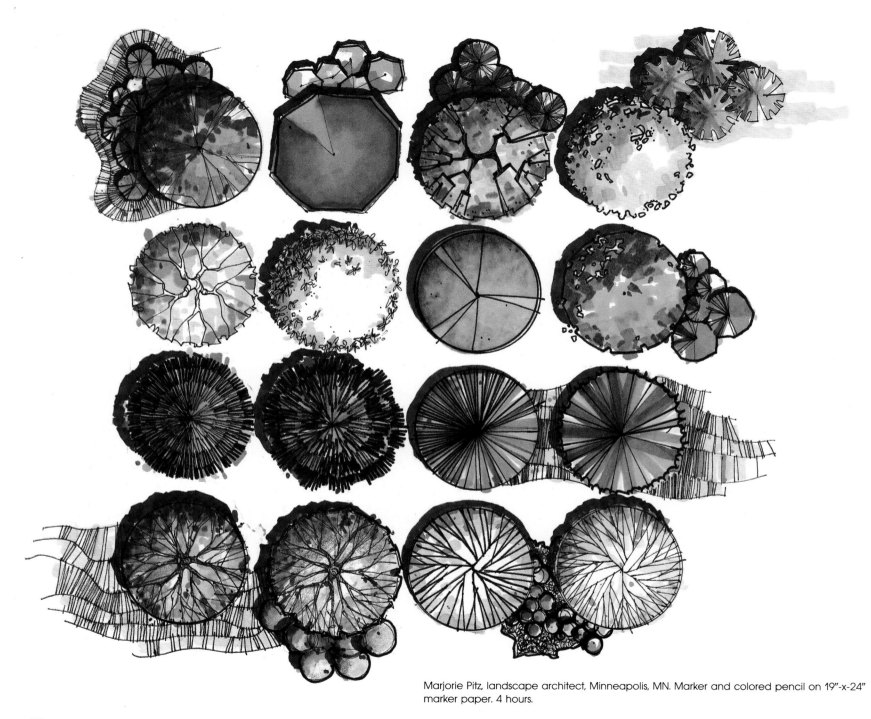

Marjorie Pitz, landscape architect, Minneapolis, MN. Marker and colored pencil on 19"-x-24" marker paper. 4 hours.

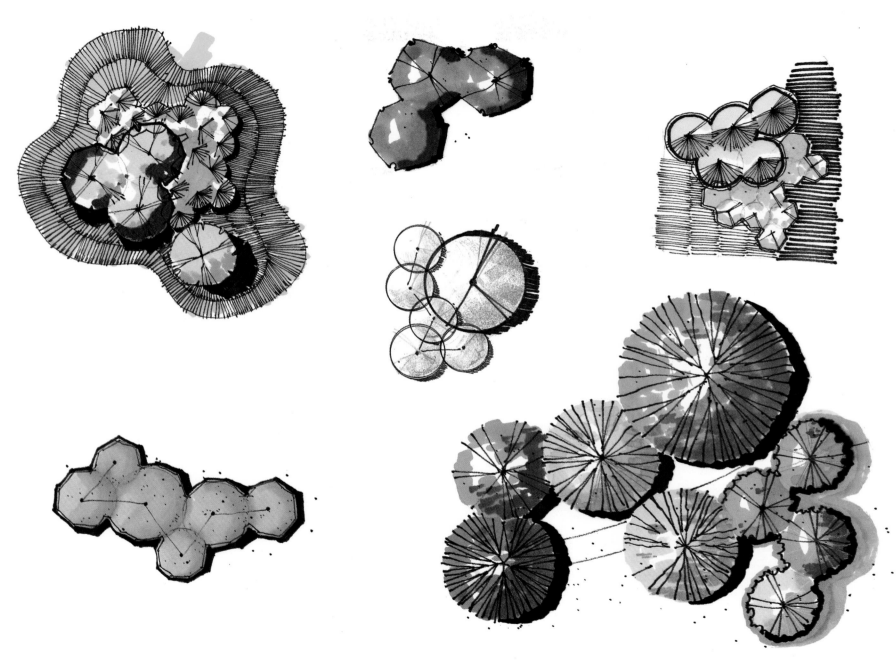

Participants, Kansas State University graphic workshop. Marker, felt-tip pen, and pastel on 19"-x-24" marker paper. 2 hours.

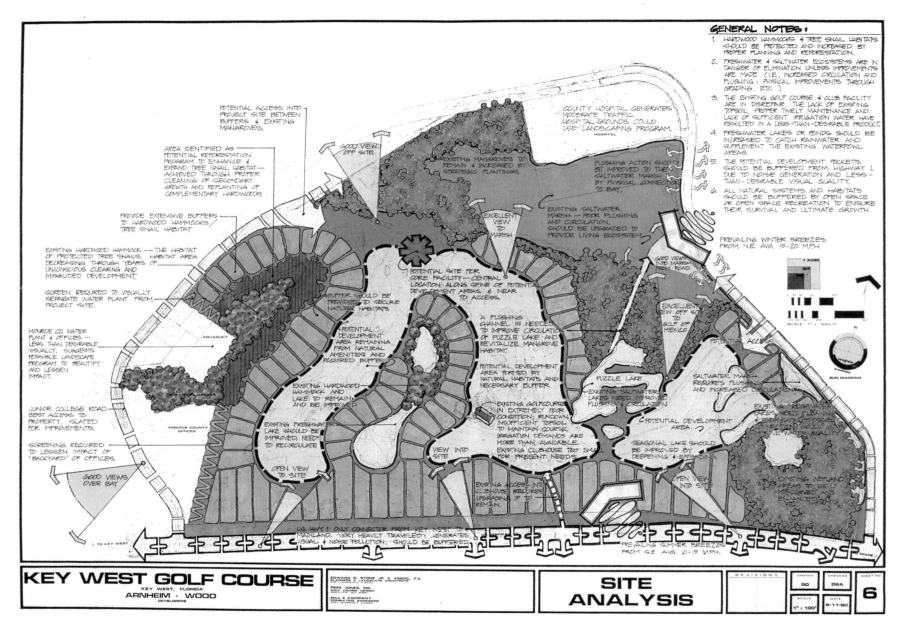

Edward D. Stone, Jr. and Associates, Fort Lauderdale, FL. Marker on 36"-x-48" black-line diazo print paper (original, ink on Mylar). 12 hours.

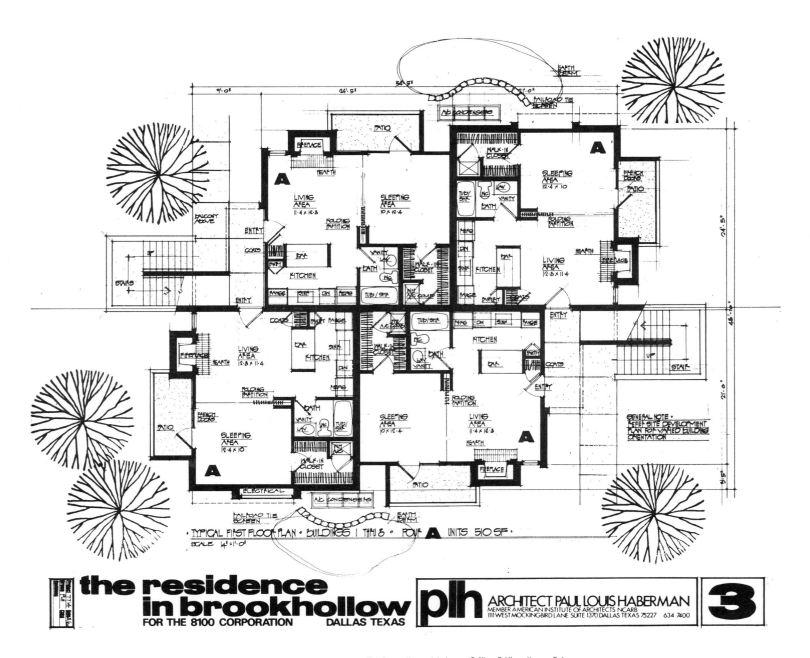

· TYPICAL FIRST FLOOR PLAN · BUILDINGS 1 THRU 8 · FOUR **A** UNITS 510 SF ·
SCALE 1/4" = 1'-0"

the residence
in brookhollow
FOR THE 8100 CORPORATION   **DALLAS TEXAS**

plh ARCHITECT PAUL LOUIS HABERMAN
MEMBER AMERICAN INSTITUTE OF ARCHITECTS N CARB
1111 WEST MOCKINGBIRD LANE SUITE 1370 DALLAS TEXAS 75227   634 7400

3

Paul Haberman, architect, Dallas, TX. Pencil and ink on 24"-x-36" vellum. 8 hours.

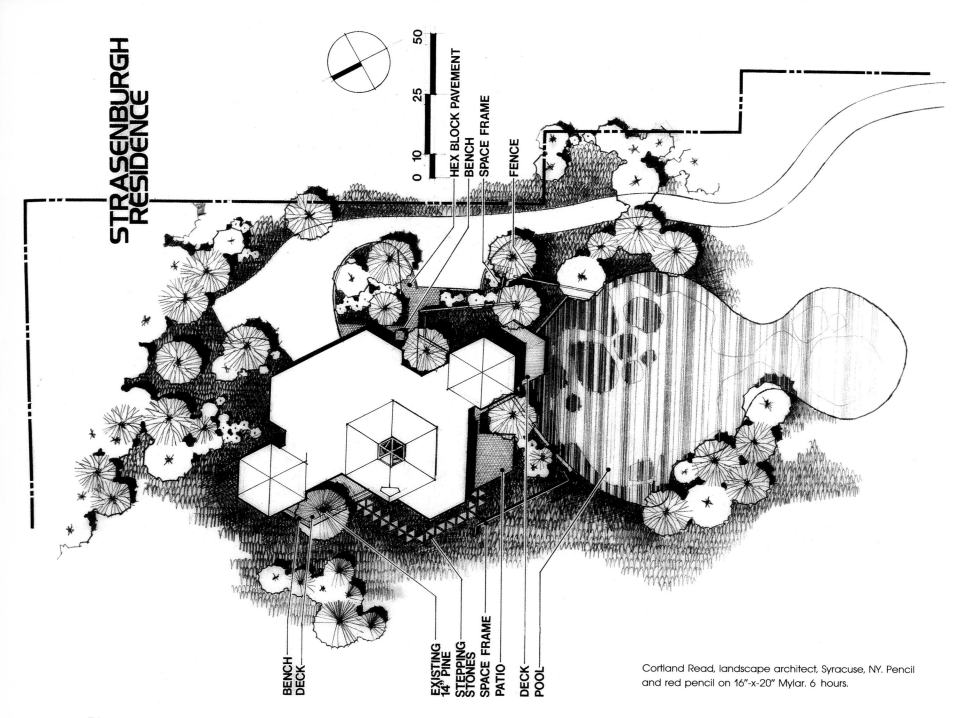

STRASENBURGH
RESIDENCE

50

25

10

0

HEX BLOCK PAVEMENT
BENCH
SPACE FRAME
FENCE

BENCH
DECK

EXISTING
14" PINE
STEPPING
STONES
SPACE FRAME
PATIO
DECK
POOL

Cortland Read, landscape architect, Syracuse, NY. Pencil
and red pencil on 16"-x-20" Mylar. 6 hours.

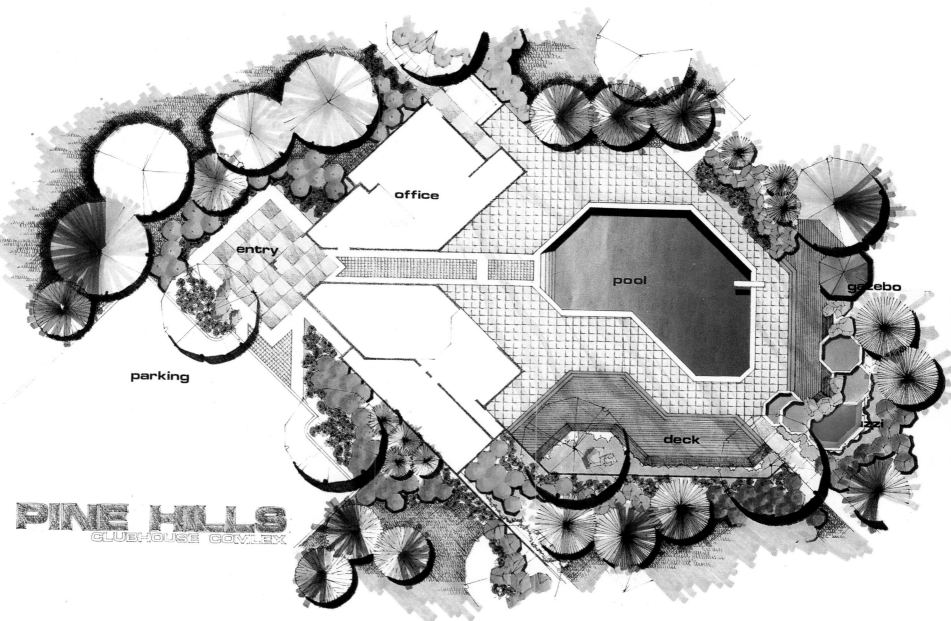

office

entry

pool

gazebo

parking

deck

zzi

PINE HILLS
CLUBHOUSE COMLEX

Tim Rorvig, student, Kansas State University. Pencil
and red colored pencil on 24"-x-36" vellum. 8
hours. (T)

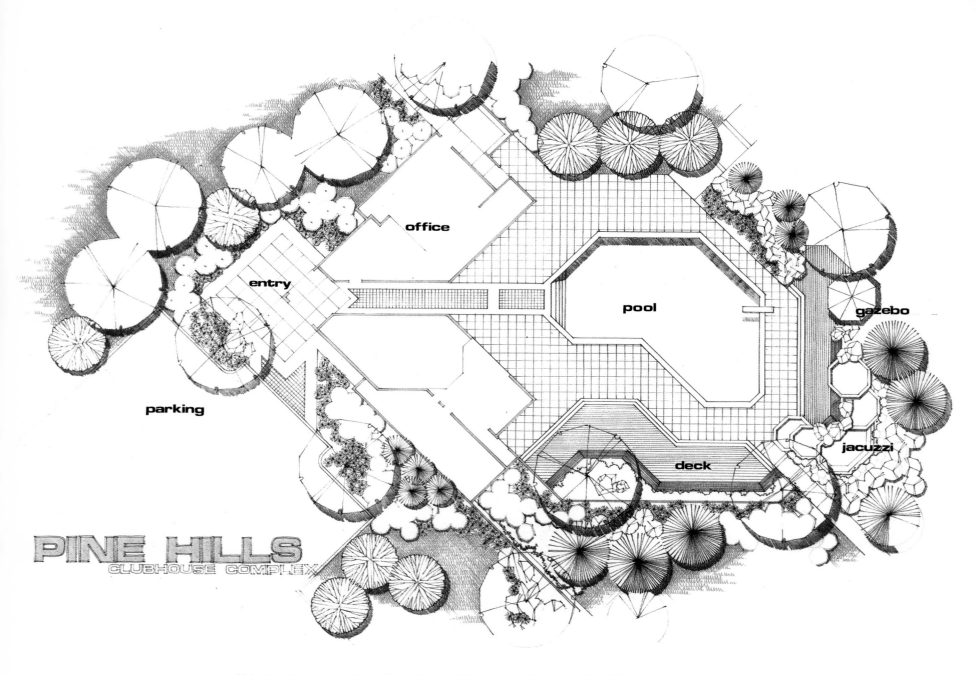

office

entry

pool

gazebo

parking

deck

jacuzzi

PINE HILLS
CLUBHOUSE COMPLEX

Libby Appling, student, Kansas State University. Marker and airbrush on 24"-x-36" blue-line print paper. 5 hours. (T)

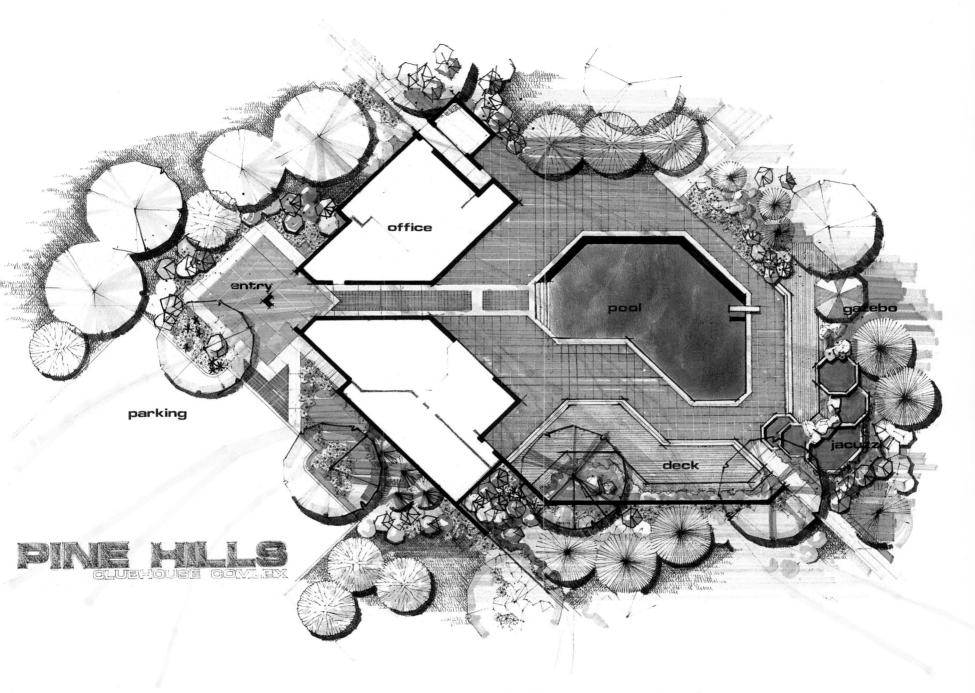

PINE HILLS
CLUBHOUSE COMPLEX

parking

entry

office

pool

gazebo

deck

jacuzzi

Ron Bork, architect, Chicago, IL. Marker and pastel on 24"-x-36" blue-line print paper. 4 hours. (T)

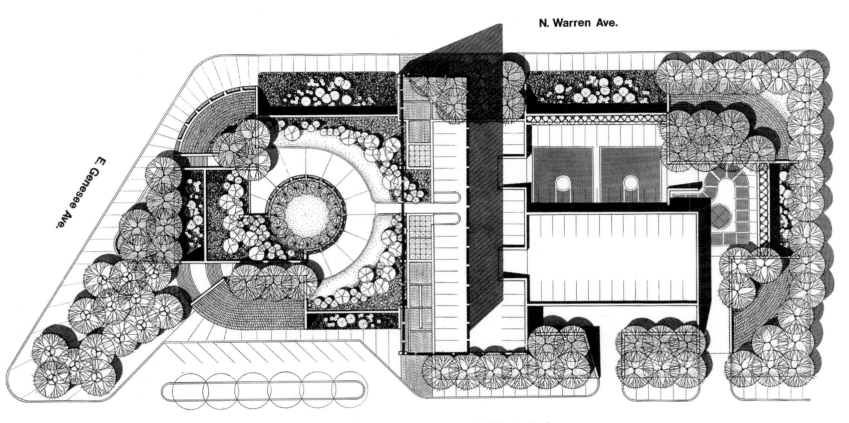

SAGINAW FEDERAL BUILDING

N. Warren Ave.

E. Genesee Ave.

N. Weadock Ave.

Johnson, Johnson, and Roy, Inc., Ann Arbor, MI. Ink on 16"-x-30" Mylar. 40 hours.

JJR
Johnson, Johnson & Roy Inc.
303 N. Main Street — Ann Arbor, Michigan 48104
Planning/Landscape Architecture
313 662-4457
Scale⁰——20
North ➡

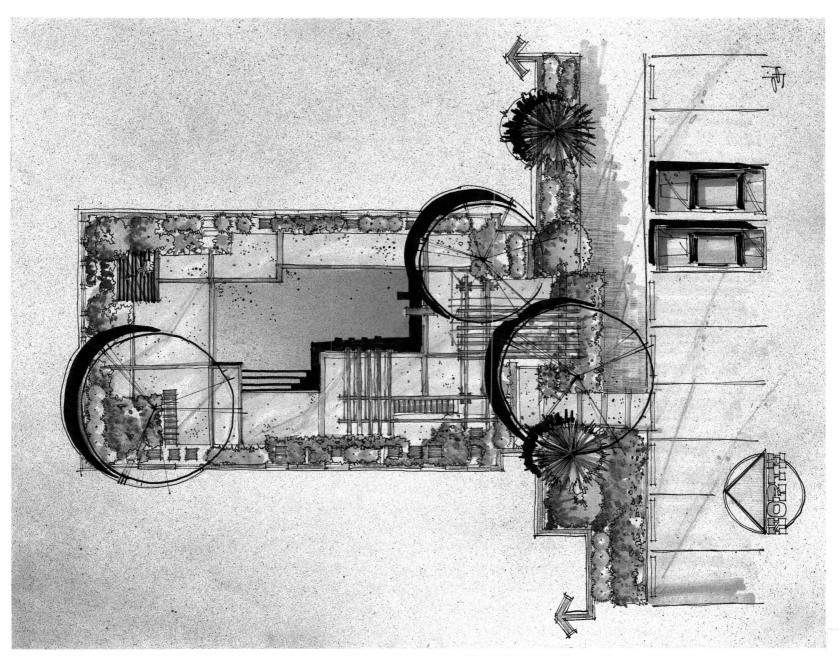

Dennis Decker, student, Kansas State University. Marker and airbrush on 16"-x-20" black-line diazo print paper. 2 hours. (T)

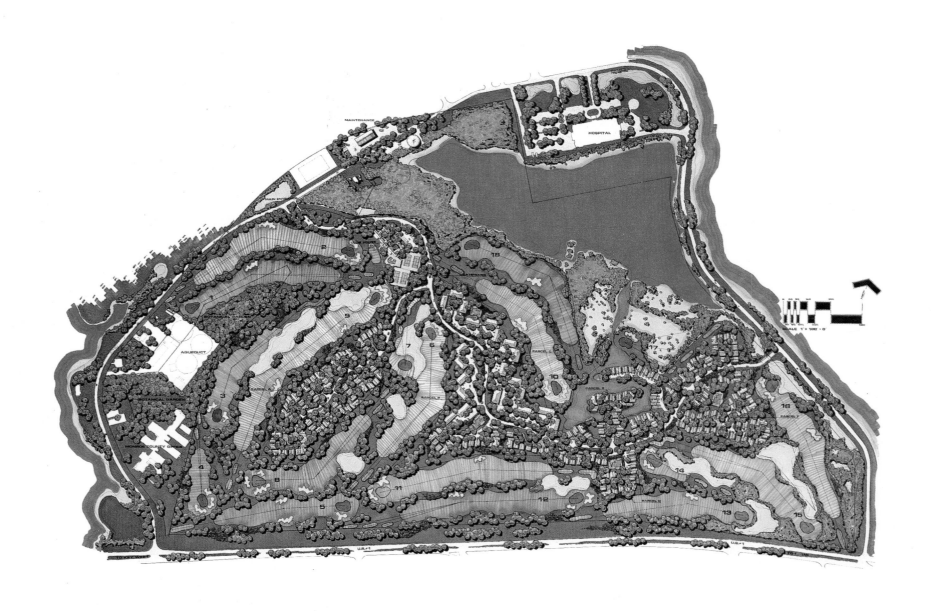

Edward D. Stone, Jr. and Associates, Fort Lauderdale, FL. Marker on 36"-x-48" black-line diazo print paper (original, pencil on Mylar). 28 hours.

Art Associates, Toledo, OH. Casein on 20"-x-24" mat-board. 60 hours.

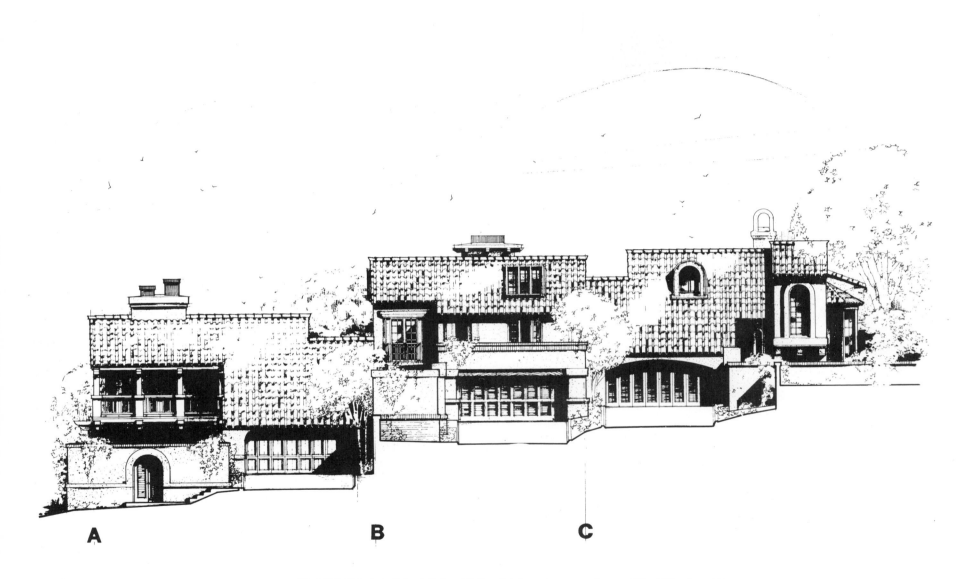

A   B   C

Paul Haberman, architect, Dallas, TX. Pencil, ink, and gray marker on 24"-x-36" vellum. 8 hours.

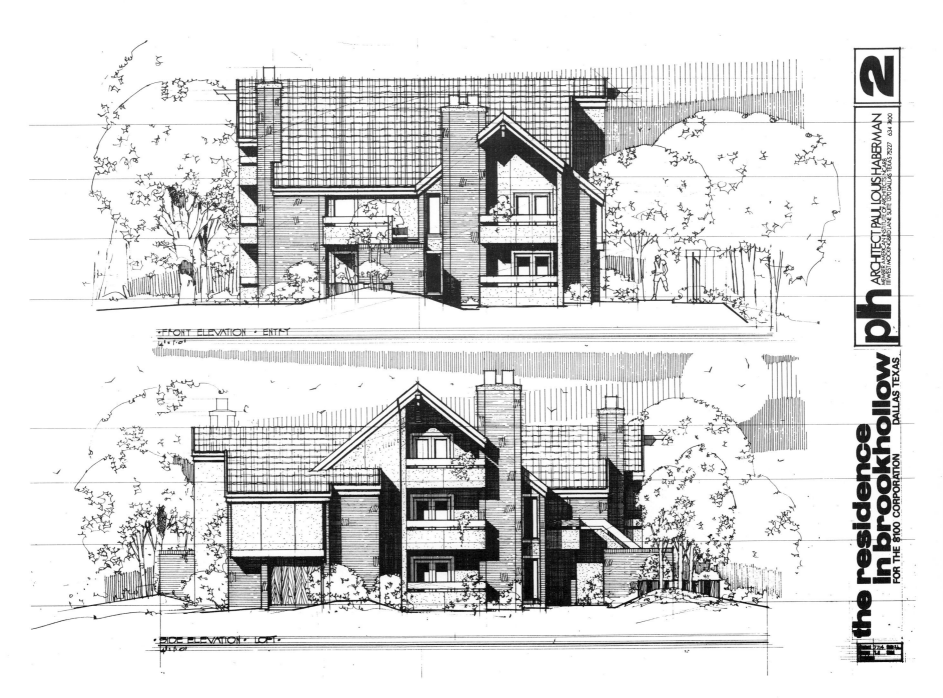

FRONT ELEVATION · ENTRY

SIDE ELEVATION · LOFT

the residence in brookhollow DALLAS TEXAS
FOR THE 8100 CORPORATION

ph ARCHITECT PAUL LOUIS HABERMAN
MEMBER AMERICAN INSTITUTE OF ARCHITECTS AIA·ARB
1111 WEST MOCKINGBIRD LANE SUITE 1370 DALLAS TEXAS 75247   634 7600

2

Paul Haberman, architect, Dallas, TX. Pencil and ink on 24"-x-36" vellum. 8 hours.

Paul Haberman, architect, Dallas, TX. Marker and ink pen on 16"-x-24" brown-line diazo print paper. 10 hours.

Participant, Kansas State University graphic workshop. Marker and felt-tip pen on 19"-x-24" marker paper. 2 hours. (T)

Robert M. Boulton, landscape architect, St. Louis, MO. Eagle 314 pencil on 16"-x-36" white tracing paper. 6 hours.

Duitsman Residence

Mike W. Lin and San-Chin Kao, architect, Taiwan. Tempera on 9"-x-15" black pastel paper. 2 hours. (T)

ELEVATION

Top: John Yancey, student, Kansas State University. Colored pencil on 10"-x-16" yellow tracing paper. 4 hours. (T) *Bottom:* San-Chin Kao, architect, Taiwan. Watercolor and colored pencil on 10"-x-16" pastel paper. 2 hours. (T)

89

Top: Kevin Kerwin, student, Kansas State University. Marker and pastel on 14"-x-24" marker paper. 3 hours. (T) *Bottom:* Bob Workman, architect, Tulsa, OK. Marker and airbrush on 14"-x-24" marker paper. 3 hours. (T)

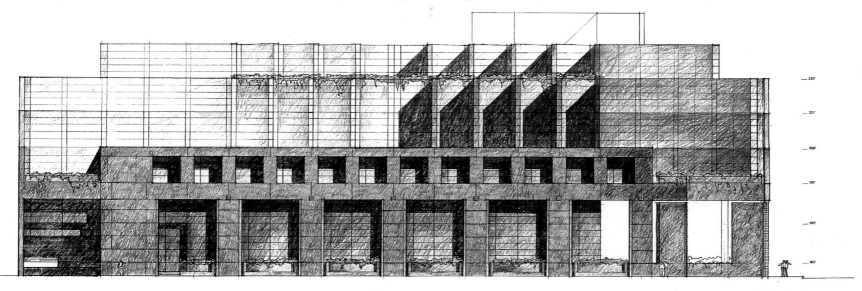

Walnut Street

Top: Fred Myers, architect, Kansas City, MO. Colored pencil on 18"-x-36" photo-mural enlargement paper (original, pencil on 9"-x-18" vellum). 7 hours. *Bottom:* Gary Mellenbruch, illustrator, Kansas City, MO. Tempera on 14"-x-30" mat-board. 12 hours.

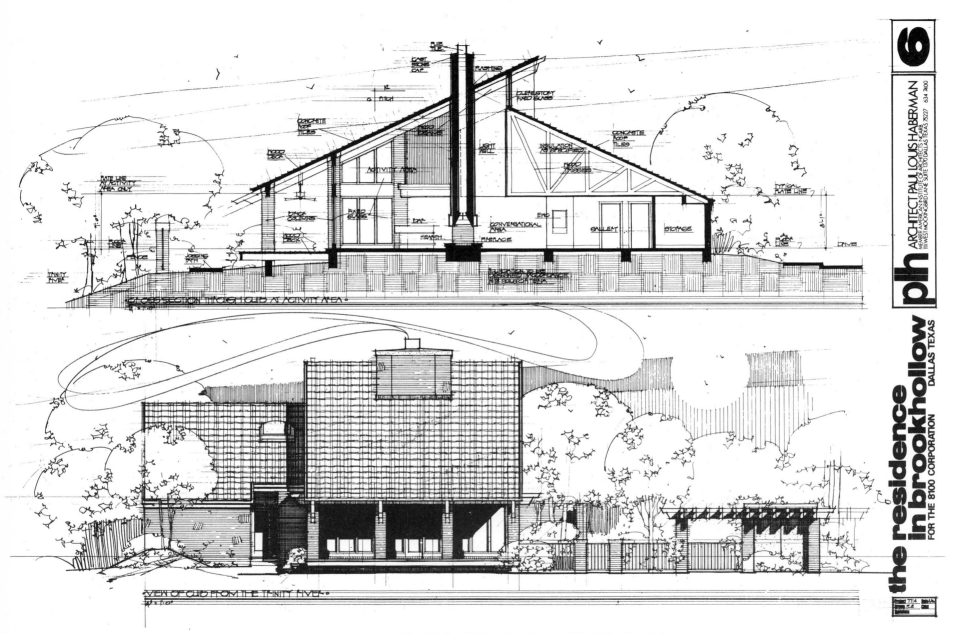

The residence in brookhollow
DALLAS TEXAS
FOR THE 8100 CORPORATION

6
ph ARCHITECT PAUL LOUIS HABERMAN
MEMBER AMERICAN INSTITUTE OF ARCHITECTS NCARB
11111 WEST MOCKINGBIRD LANE SUITE 1370 DALLAS TEXAS 75227   634 7400

Paul Haberman, architect, Dallas, TX. Pencil and ink on 24"-x-36" vellum. 8 hours.

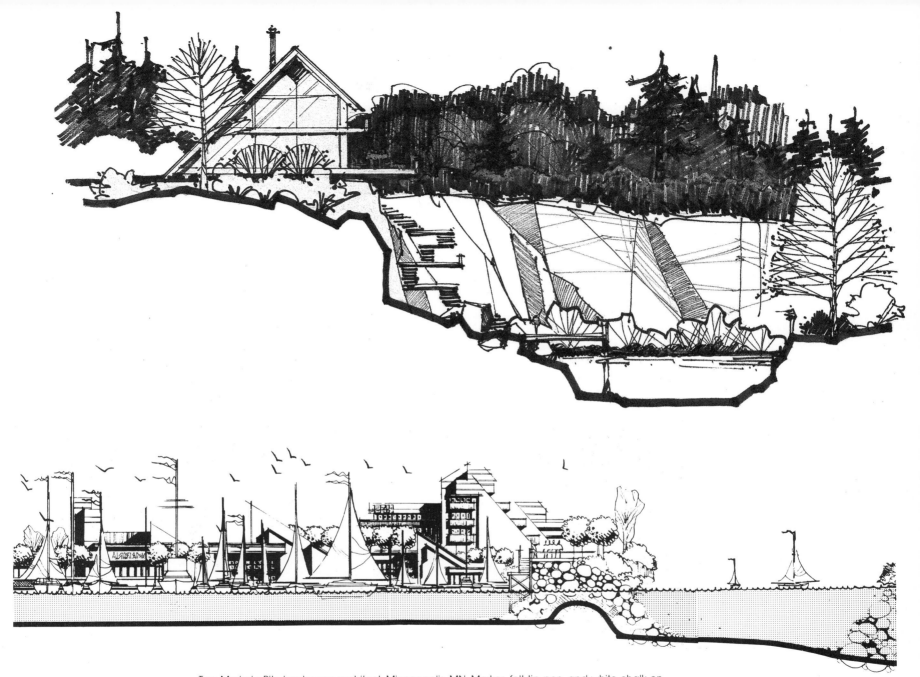

Top: Marjorie Pitz, landscape architect, Minneapolis, MN. Marker, felt-tip pen, and white chalk on 18"-x-24" newsprint paper. 2 hours. *Bottom:* Architect Engineer Design Group, West Palm Beach, FL. Pencil on 12"-x-60" vellum. 8 hours.

VIEWS to PARK

LAKESIDE

LOUNGE/MEETING RM.

422   DROP OFF

401

CONCEPT E
ALTERNATIVE Z.

Johnson, Johnson, and Roy, Inc., Ann Arbor, MI. Marker and felt-tip pen. *Top:* 6"-x-12" white tracing paper. ½ hour. *Bottom:* 12"-x-28" white tracing paper. 2 hours.

Dennis Decker, student, Kansas State University. Marker and tempera on 19"-x-24" marker paper. 3 hours. (T)

Leslie Carow, student, Colorado State University. Marker and airbrush on 19"-x-24" marker paper. 4 hours.

Robert Workman, architect, Tulsa, OK. Marker, white tempera, and colored pencil on 19"-x-24" marker paper. 4 hours.

LOOSE SKETCHES

4

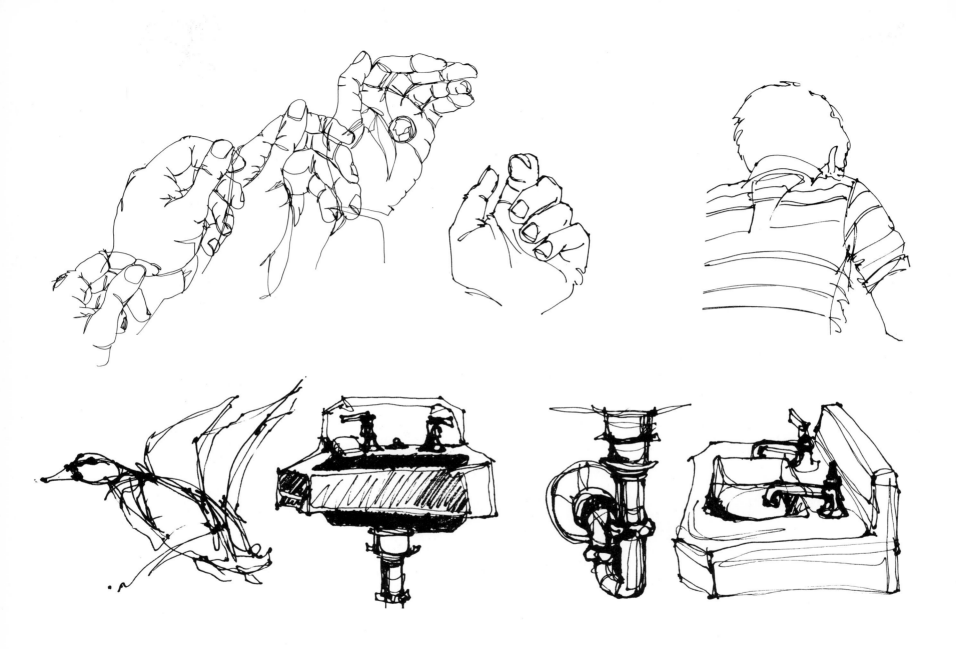

Participants, Kansas State University graphic workshop. *Top:* Sharpie pen on 10"-x-28" bond paper.
Bottom: paper towel. 2 to 4 minutes each.

Top left: Dick Sneary, illustrator, Kansas City, MO. Black marker on 19"-x-24" marker paper. 10 minutes. *Top right:* Tee Hung Tan, student, Kansas State University. 6B carpenter pencil on 8"-x-10" bond paper. 10 minutes. *Bottom:* Thomas Wang, professor, University of Michigan. Marker on 6"-x-14" marker paper. 3 minutes.

Ron Bork, architect, Chicago, IL. 6B carpenter pencil on 19"-x-24" marker paper. 1 hour.

Thomas Wang, professor, University of Michigan. 6B carpenter pencil and colored pencil on 16"-x- 20" marker paper. 40 minutes.

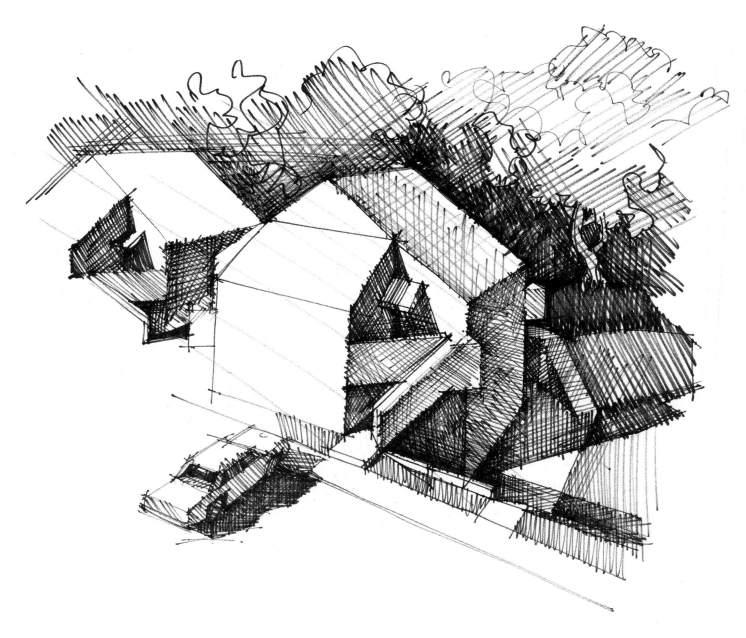

Dick Sneary, illustrator, Kansas City, MO. Sharpie pen on 18"-x-22" marker paper. 40 minutes. (T)

Dick Sneary, illustrator, Kansas City, MO. *Left:* Sharpie pen on 8½"-x-11" bond paper, 15 minutes. (T)
Right: Colored pencil and pastel on 20"-x-30" vellum. 30 minutes.

Fiskebäckskil/Sw.
P. Laseau

E. Fiskebäckskil/Sw.
P. Laseau

Paul Laseau, professor, Ball State University. Felt-tip pen and colored pencil on 8"-x-10" bristol paper. 30 minutes each.

Entry/Buckingham Palace

Le Sevigne

Paul Laseau, professor, Ball State University. Felt-tip pen and colored pencil on 10"-x-14" bristol paper. 15 to 30 minutes each.

Mike W. Lin. Black chalk on 19"-x-24" marker paper. 1 minute.

Mike W. Lin. Pastel on 12"-x-16" bond paper. 10 minutes.

Dick Sneary, illustrator, Kansas City, MO. Pastel and colored pencil on 19"-x-24" marker paper. 1 hour.

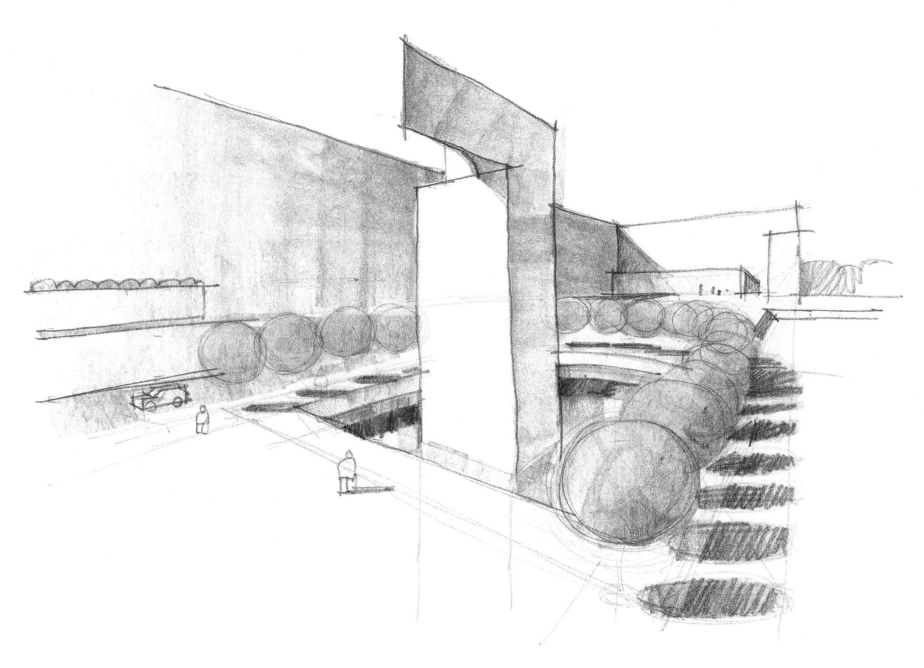

Dick Sneary, illustrator, Kansas City, MO. Pastel and colored pencil on 18"-x-24" marker paper. 30 minutes. (T)

Chris Barna, landscape architect, NC. Pastel and colored pencil on 18"-x-24" yellow tracing paper. 1½ hours.

Charlotte Kinderknecht, student, Kansas State University. Sharpie pen on 14"-x-22" yellow tracing paper (using slide projection). 1½ hours.

Loke Low, student, Kansas State University. Marker and felt-tip pen on 12"-x-18" yellow tracing paper. 40 minutes.

Wayne Williams, professor, Washington State University. Marker, pastel, and colored pencil on 14"-x-19" yellow tracing paper. 1 hour.

Left: Theresa O'Connell, student, Kansas State University. *Right:* Marjorie Pitz, landscape architect, Minneapolis, MN. Marker and colored pencil on 10"-x-12" yellow tracing paper. 40 minutes each. (T)

Michael E. Doyle, illustrator, Boulder, CO. Marker and colored pencil on 8"-x-10" bond paper. 1½ hours.

Liza Ermeling, student, Kansas State University. Marker and colored pencil on 19"-x-24" marker paper. 40 minutes.

Left: Marjorie Pitz, landscape architect, Minneapolis, MN. Felt-tip pen and marker on 11"-x-14" rice paper. 40 minutes. *Right:* Tim McNamara, student, Kansas State University. Marker on 12"-x-14" rice paper. 25 minutes.

Mike W. Lin. Marker, pastel, and airbrush on 19"-x-24" marker paper. 20 minutes total: 5 minutes blindfolded, 15 minutes without blindfold.

Thomas Wang, professor, University of Michigan. Watercolor and Sharpie pen on 14"-x-16" watercolor paper. ½ hour.

Thomas Wang, professor, University of Michigan. Marker on 16"-x-24" marker paper. 40 minutes each.

Thomas Wang, professor, University of Michigan. Marker on 12"-x-16" (top), 10"-x-18" (bottom) marker
paper. 40 minutes each.

Thomas Wang, professor, University of Michigan. *Left:* Felt-tip black marker and watercolor on 13"-x-14" rice paper. 45 minutes. *Right:* Felt-tip pen and colored Zipatone on 8"-x-10" bristol paper. 45 minutes.

EXTERIOR
ILLUSTRATIONS

5

Left: Robert Boulton, landscape architect, St. Louis, MO. Eagle #314 pencil on 10"-x-14" vellum. 1 hour. *Right:* Anne Hunt, student, England. Colored pencil on 11"-x-14" vellum. 1 hour.

Carl Johnson, landscape architect, Ann Arbor, MI. Pencil on 9"-x-12" bond paper. 30 minutes each.

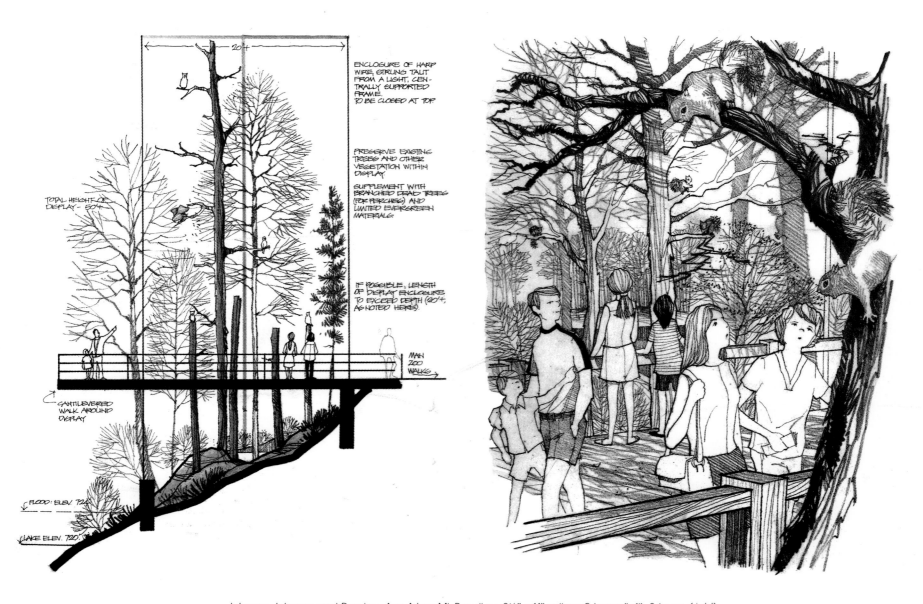

ENCLOSURE OF HARP
WIRE, STRUNG TAUT
FROM A LIGHT, CEN-
TRALLY SUPPORTED
FRAME.
TO BE CLOSED AT TOP

PRESERVE EXISTING
TREES AND OTHER
VEGETATION WITHIN
DISPLAY

SUPPLEMENT WITH
BRANCHED DEAD TREES
(FOR PERCHES) AND
LIMITED EVERGREEN
MATERIALS

IF POSSIBLE, LENGTH
OF DISPLAY ENCLOSURE
TO EXCEED DEPTH (20'±,
AS NOTED HERE)

TOTAL HEIGHT OF
DISPLAY - 50'±

20'±

MAIN
ZOO
WALKS

CANTILEVERED
WALK AROUND
DISPLAY

FLOOD ELEV. 724±

LAKE ELEV. 720±

Johnson, Johnson, and Roy, Inc., Ann Arbor, MI. Pencil on 8½"-x-11" vellum. 2 hours (left), 3 hours (right).

128

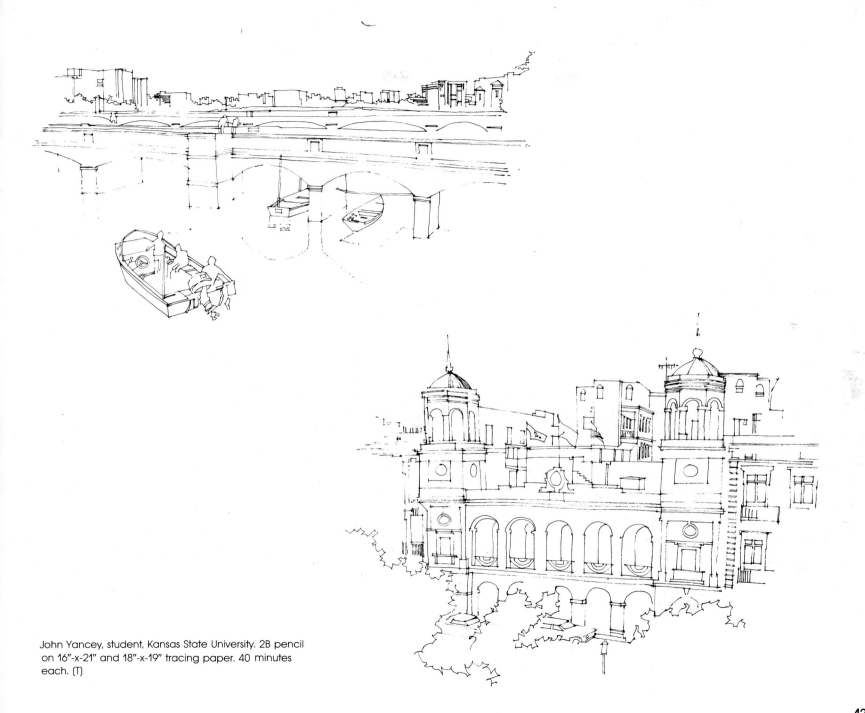

John Yancey, student, Kansas State University. 2B pencil on 16"-x-21" and 18"-x-19" tracing paper. 40 minutes each. (T)

Craig Patterson, architect, Kansas City, MO. Pencil on 16"-x-20" vellum. 6 hours.

Cortland Read, landscape architect, Syracuse, NY. Pencil and red pencil on 16"-x-20" Mylar. 8 hours, from slide.

Jim Hayes, illustrator, Honolulu, HI. Carbon pencil on 12"-x-18" vellum. 12 hours.

Jim Hayes, illustrator, Honolulu, Hl. Carbon pencil on 12"-x-20" vellum. 12 hours.

Jim Hayes, illustrator, Honolulu, HI. Carbon pencil on 20"-x-30" vellum. 24 hours.

Donald Hilderbrandt, landscape architect, Columbia, MD. No. 2 Berol Mirado pencil on 18"-x-24" vellum. 16 hours.

Donald Hilderbrandt, landscape architect, Columbia, MD. No. 2 Berol Mirado pencil on 16"-x-30" vellum. 16 hours.

Donald Hilderbrandt, landscape architect, Columbia, MD. No. 2 Berol Mirado pencil on 18"-x-24" vellum. 10 hours.

Robert Boulton, landscape architect, St. Louis, MO. Eagle #314 on 17"-x-22" yellow tracing paper. 3 hours.

Art Associates, Toledo, OH. Pencil on 20"-x-30" Crescent board. 15 hours.

ROSSON HOUSE · PHOENIX   R. JONES 83

Robert Jones, architect, Topeka, KS. Felt-tip pen on 8"-x-10" yellow tracing paper. 2½ hours.

Carol Johnson, landscape architect, Ann Arbor, MI. Ink on 4"-x-6" marker paper. 30 minutes each.

Denny Potts, student, Kansas State University. No. 00 ink pen on 12"-x-18" vellum. 5 hours. (T)

Dick Sneary, illustrator, Kansas City, MO. Ink pen on 10"-x-14" vellum. 4 hours.

Dick Sneary, illustrator, Kansas City, MO. Sharpie pen on 19"-x-24" vellum. 1 hour. (T)

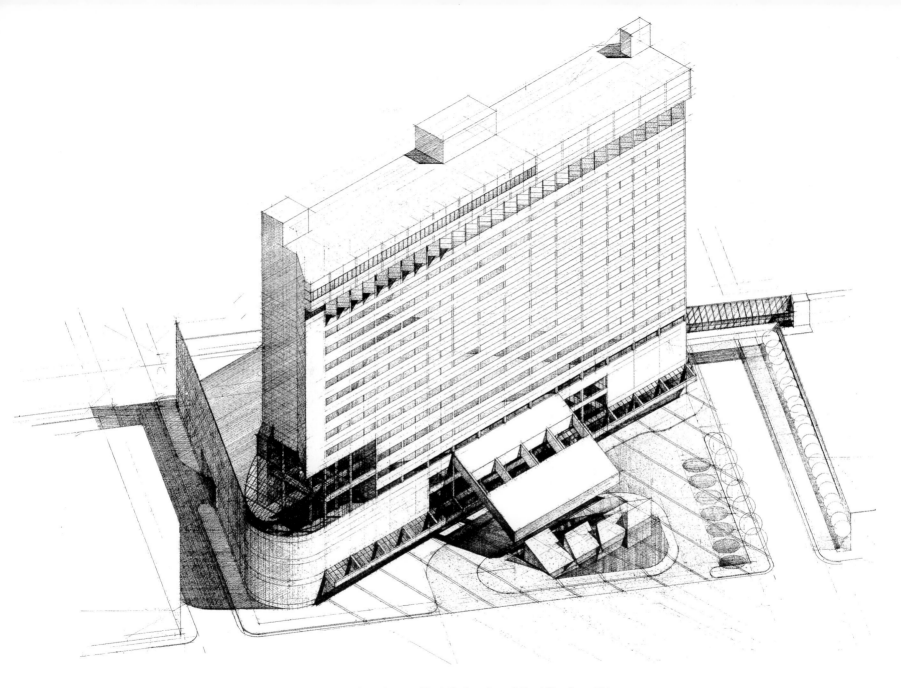

Dick Sneary, architect, Kansas City, MO. Pencil on 24"-x-30" vellum. 10 hours.

Rod Henmi, professor, Washington University. Fountain pen and ink wash on 16"-x-20" watercolor paper. 5 hours.

146

Jan. 5, 1978 Grandpa Hidekawa's house - Tamashima

Rod Henmi, professor, Washington University. Fountain pen and ink wash on 16"-x-20" watercolor paper. 7 hours.

Gene Streett, illustrator, Chicago, IL. Ink pen on 20"-x-30" vellum. 28 hours.

Kevin Karst, student, Kansas State University. Pastel and black colored pencil on 19"-x-24" marker
paper. 5 hours.

Dick Sneary, illustrator, Kansas City, MO. Pastel and colored pencil on 19"-x-24" vellum. 1 hour. (T)

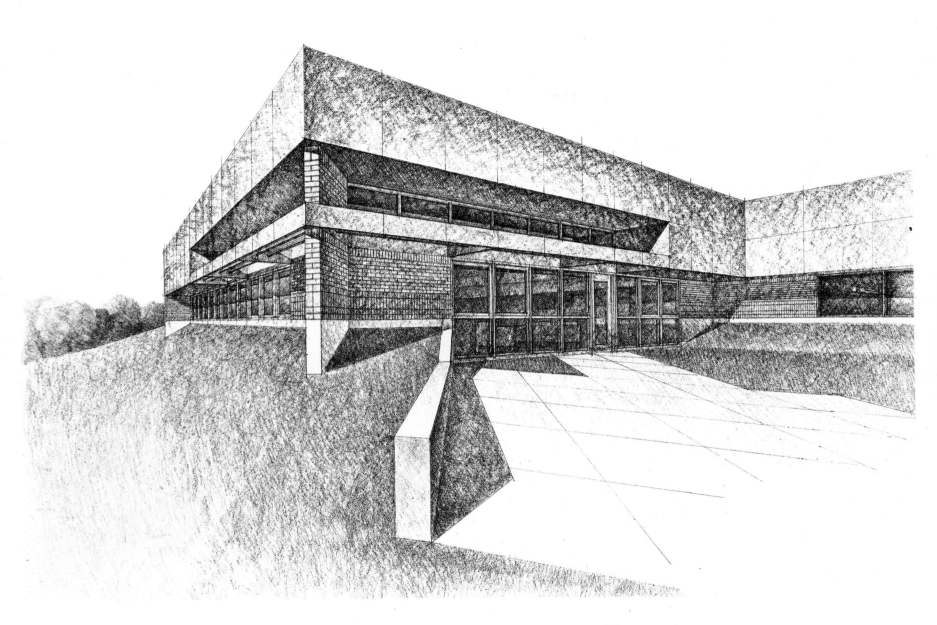

Dick Sneary, illustrator, Kansas City, MO. Pastel and colored pencil on 30"-x-42" photo-mural enlargement paper (original, pencil on 10"-x-12" vellum). 12 hours.

Dick Sneary, illustrator, Kansas City, MO. Ink and colored pencil on 18"-x-28" yellow tracing paper. 15 hours.

Dick Sneary, architect, Kansas City, MO. Pastel and colored pencil on 18"-x-24" yellow tracing paper. 16 hours.

Dick Sneary, architect, Kansas City, MO. Pastel and colored pencil on 24"-x-24" yellow tracing paper. 5 hours.

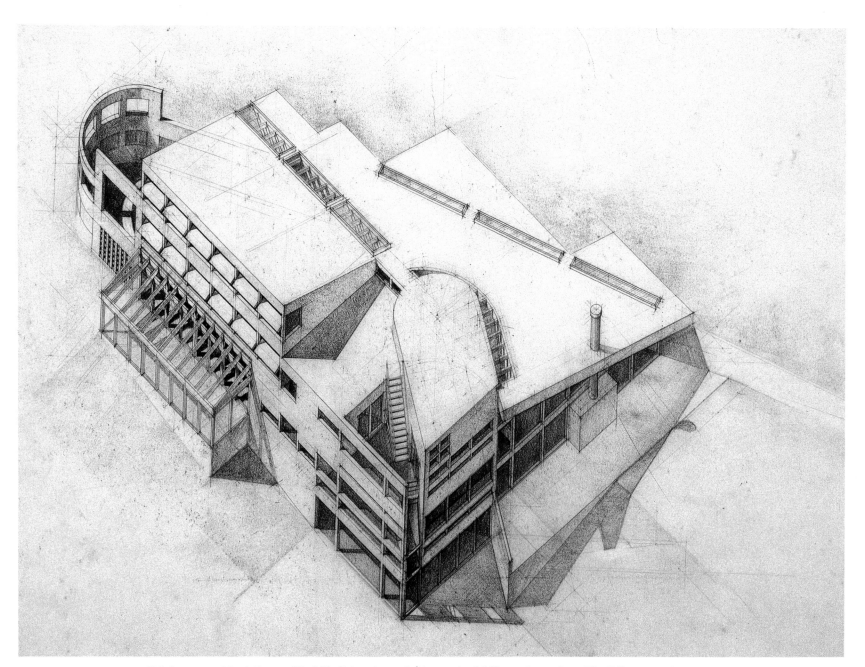

Dick Sneary, architect, Kansas City, MO. Colored pencil, Prismacolor Art Stix, and pencil on 19"-x-24" vellum. 10 hours.

STUDY of "IL GAZETTINO"
CAMPO SANTA APONALE
VENICE, ITALY
30 APRIL 1982

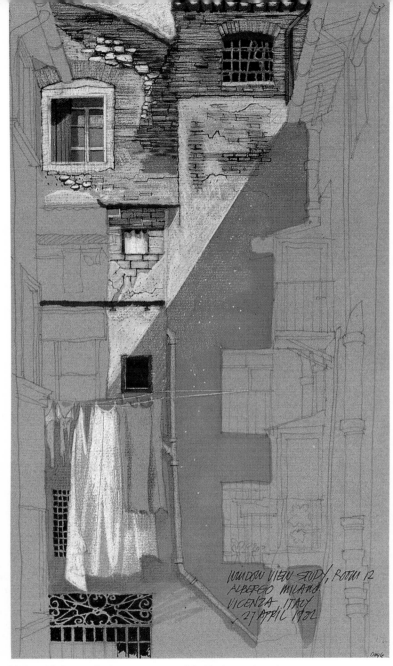

WINDOW VIEW STUDY, ROOM 12
ALBERGO MILANO
VICENZA, ITALY
27 APRIL 1982

Michael E. Doyle, illustrator, Boulder, CO. Marker, colored pencil, and pencil on 9"-x-15" pastel paper. 2 hours each.

Michael E. Doyle, illustrator, Boulder, CO. Marker and colored pencil on 9"-x-9" black-line diazo print paper (original, felt-tip pen on yellow tracing paper). 1 hour each.

Michael E. Doyle, illustrator, Boulder, CO. Marker and colored pencil on 10"-x-13" pastel paper. 2 hours.

Leslie Carow, student, Colorado State University. Marker, colored pencil, and airbrush on 19"-x-24" marker paper. 10 hours.

Kurtis Robinson, student, Kansas State University. Marker on 12"-x-12" rice paper. 1½ hours. (T)

Craig Roberts, illustrator, Ft. Lauderdale, FL. Marker on 24"-x-30" rice paper. 8 hours.

Craig Roberts, illustrator, Ft. Lauderdale, FL. Marker on 24"-x-30" rice paper. 7½ hours.

Craig Roberts, illustrator, Ft. Lauderdale, FL. Marker on 24"-x-36" rice paper. 7 hours.

Paul Haberman, architect, Dallas, TX. Marker, Sharpie pen, and pencil on 24"-x-36" yellow tracing paper. 2 hours.

Paul Haberman, architect, Dallas, TX. Marker, ink pen, and pencil on 16"-x-20" yellow tracing paper. 4 hours.

Paul Haberman, architect, Dallas, TX. Marker, ink pen, pencil, and white pencil on 16"-x-32" yellow tracing paper. 14 hours.

Jim Hayes, illustrator, Honolulu, HI. Marker on 20"-x-30" black-line diazo print paper (original, carbon pencil on vellum). 20 hours.

Jim Hayes, illustrator, Honolulu, HI. Marker and pastel on 24"-x-36" black-line diazo print paper (original, carbon pencil on vellum). 24 hours.

Jim Hayes, illustrator, Honolulu, HI. Marker on 24"-x-36" black-line diazo print paper (original, carbon pencil on vellum). 32 hours.

Jim Hayes, illustrator, Honolulu, Hl. Marker on 24"-x-36" black-line diazo print paper (original, carbon pencil on vellum). 27 hours.

Johnson, Johnson, and Roy, Inc., Ann Arbor, MI. Marker on 16"-x-24" photo-mural enlargement paper (original, pencil on 11"-x-17" tracing paper). 20 hours.

Angela Budano-Mucciolo, Bacci Design, Boynton Beach, FL. Marker and pastel on 24"-x-36" black-line diazo print paper (original, felt-tip pen on sepia paper). 25 hours.

Mike W. Lin. Marker, tempera, colored pencil, and pastel on 19"-x-24" marker paper. 14 hours.

Mike W. Lin. Marker, tempera, colored pencil, and pastel on 19"-x-24" marker paper. 14 hours.

Gene Streett, illustrator, Chicago, IL. Marker, ink, and airbrush on 16"-x-30" watercolor board. 22 hours.

Gene Streett, illustrator, Chicago, IL. Marker and airbrush on 16"-x-30 black-line diazo print paper (original, ink on vellum). 24 hours.

Gene Streett, illustrator, Chicago, IL. Marker, airbrush, and white tempera on 20"-x-30" black-line
diazo print paper (original, ink on vellum). 32 hours.

Gene Streett, illustrator, Chicago, IL. Marker, airbrush, and white tempera on 20"-x-30" black-line diazo print paper (original, ink on vellum). 32 hours.

Motoomi & Associates, Honolulu, HI. *Top sheet:* Acrylic on back of 24"-x-30" printed acetate film.
Bottom sheet: Watercolor on watercolor board. 40 hours total.

Dick Sneary, illustrator, Kansas City, MO. Marker on 30"-x-40" sepia print paper (original, ink on vellum). 60 hours.

181

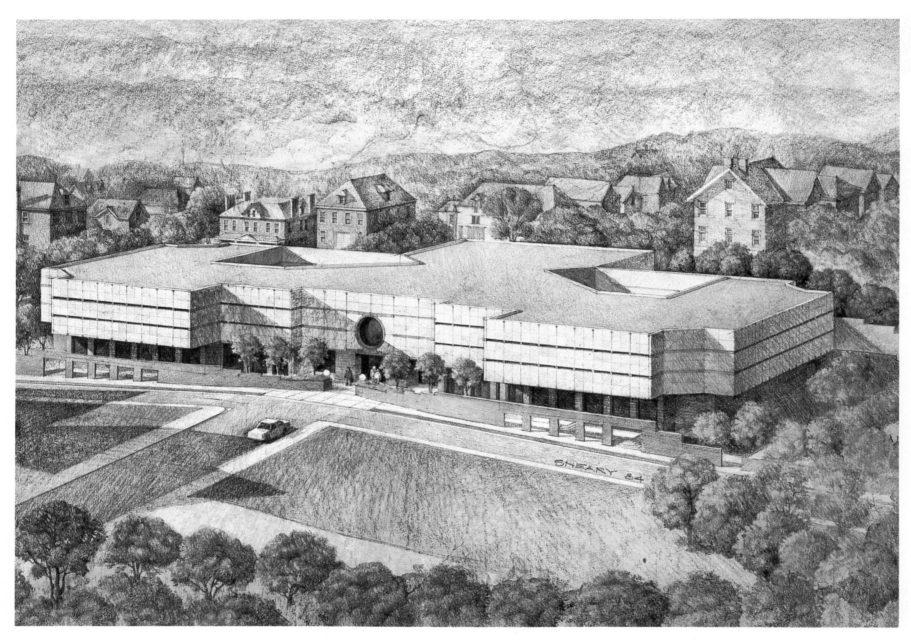

Dick Sneary, illustrator, Kansas City, MO. Watercolor, colored pencil, and art Stix on 15"-x-33" black-line diazo print paper (original, pencil on vellum). 30 hours.

Left: John Yancey, student, Kansas State University. Felt-tip pen, marker, and white colored pen on 14"-x-16" yellow tracing paper, mounted over brown paper. 6 hours. (T) *Right:* Rex Barber, student, Kansas State University. Acrylic, on the back of 18"-x-24" Mylar acetate film (original, ink on vellum). 22 hours. (T)

Marshall Associates, Dallas, TX. *Top sheet:* Acrylic painted on the back of printed acetate film.
Bottom sheet: Marker and pastel on 18"-x-40" vellum. 32 hours total.

MARSHALL & ASSOC.

Edwin Pointer, illustrator, Wichita, KS. Acrylic and felt-tip pen on 12"-x-20" watercolor board, 12 hours.

Edwin Pointer, illustrator, Wichita, KS. Acrylic and ink pen on 15"-x-18" Crescent 100 board. 17 hours.

Carlos Diniz Associates, Los Angeles, CA. Acrylic on 8"-x-8" photo-mural paper (original, ink on vellum). 20 hours each.

Carlos Diniz Associates, Los Angeles, CA. Acrylic on 8"-x-8" photo-mural paper (original, ink on vellum). 28 hours each.

193

Carlos Diniz Associates, Los Angeles, CA. Acrylic on 23"-x-32" photo-mural paper (original, ink on vellum). 225 hours.

Carlos Diniz Associates, Los Angeles, CA. *Left:* Acrylic on 19"-x-26" photo-mural paper. 220 hours.
Right: Acrylic and oil on 20"-x-34" photo-mural paper. 335 hours.

Doran Barham, illustrator, Wichita, KS. Watercolor on 16"-x-24" watercolor paper. 6 hours (left), 16 hours (right).

Stanley Dudek, artist, Chicago, IL. Watercolor on 10"-x-12" watercolor paper. 2 hours.

George Holton, student, Kansas State University. Watercolor and pencil on 10"-x-15" watercolor paper. 2 hours.

Thomas Wang, professor, University of Michigan. Watercolor, black marker, and felt-tip pen on 15"-x-22" watercolor paper. 1½ hours.

Thomas Wang, professor, University of Michigan. Watercolor, felt-tip pen, and pencil on 12″-x-20″
watercolor paper. 1 hour.

Thomas Wang, professor, University of Michigan. Watercolor and felt-tip pen on 12"-x-18"
watercolor paper. 2 hours.

Doran Barham, illustrator, Wichita, KS. Watercolor and ink pen on 12"-x-16" watercolor board. 16 hours.

Doran Barham, illustrator, Wichita, KS. Watercolor and ink pen on 12"-x-16" watercolor board. 18 hours.

Doran Barham, illustrator, Wichita, KS. Watercolor on 12"-x-16" watercolor board. 8 hours each.

204

Tran Gia Khiem, illustrator, Los Angeles, CA. Watercolor on 24"-x-36" art-sepia paper. 5 hours.

Gary Mellenbruch, illustrator, Kansas City, MO. Tempera on 16"-x-30" Crescent 100 illustration board. 18 hours.

Gary Mellenbruch, illustrator, Kansas City, MO. Tempera on 16"-x-30" mat-board. 20 hours.

Art Associates, Toledo, OH. Casein on 18"-x-14" mat-board. 12 hours.

Art Associates, Toledo, OH. Casein on 18"-x-26" Crescent 100 board. 50 hours.

Art Associates, Toledo, OH. Casein on 16"-x-28" mat-board. 60 hours.

Art Associates, Toledo, OH. Casein on 16"-x-24" mat-board. 50 hours.

Art Associates, Toledo, OH. Casein on 18"-x-36" mat-board. 70 hours.

Mike W. Lin. Tempera on 20"-x-30" Crescent 100 illustration board. 25 hours.

Gary Mellenbruch, illustrator, Kansas City, MO. Tempera on 20"-x-30" mat-board. 24 hours.

Gary Mellenbruch, illustrator, Kansas City, MO. Tempera on 20"-x-30" mat-board. 24 hours.

Dick Sneary, illustrator, Kansas City, MO. Airbrush on 16"-x-24" sepia print (original, ink on vellum). 50 hours.

Dick Sneary, illustrator, Kansas City, MO. Airbrush on 16"-x-24" sepia print (original, ink on vellum). 50 hours.

Dick Sneary, illustrator, Kansas City, MO. Airbrush on 14"-x-26" sepia print (original, ink on vellum). 50 hours.

Doran Barham, illustrator, Wichita, KS. Watercolor and ink pen on 16"-x-28" watercolor board. 22 hours.

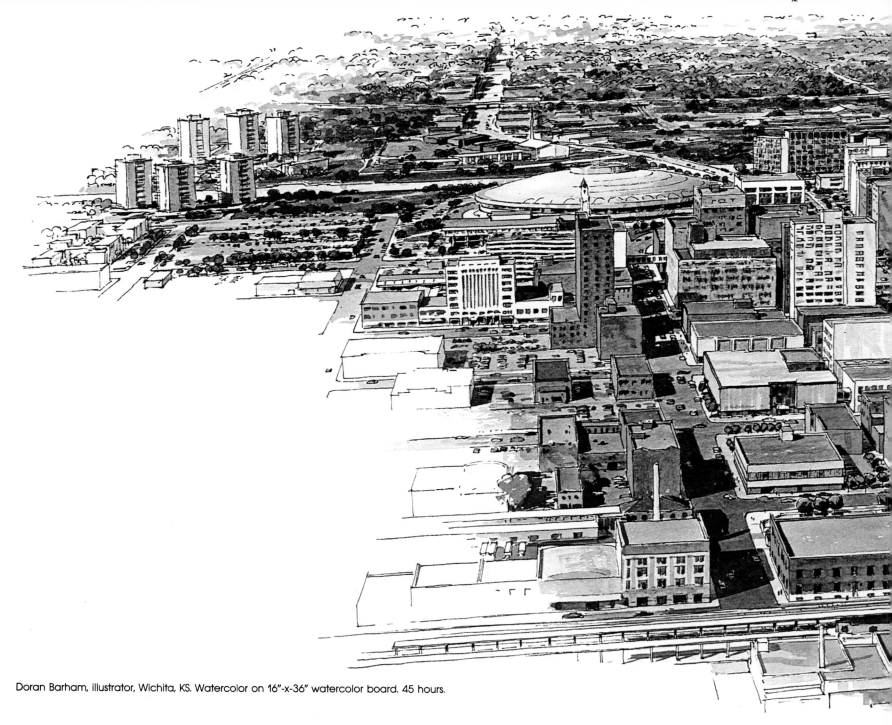

Doran Barham, illustrator, Wichita, KS. Watercolor on 16"-x-36" watercolor board. 45 hours.

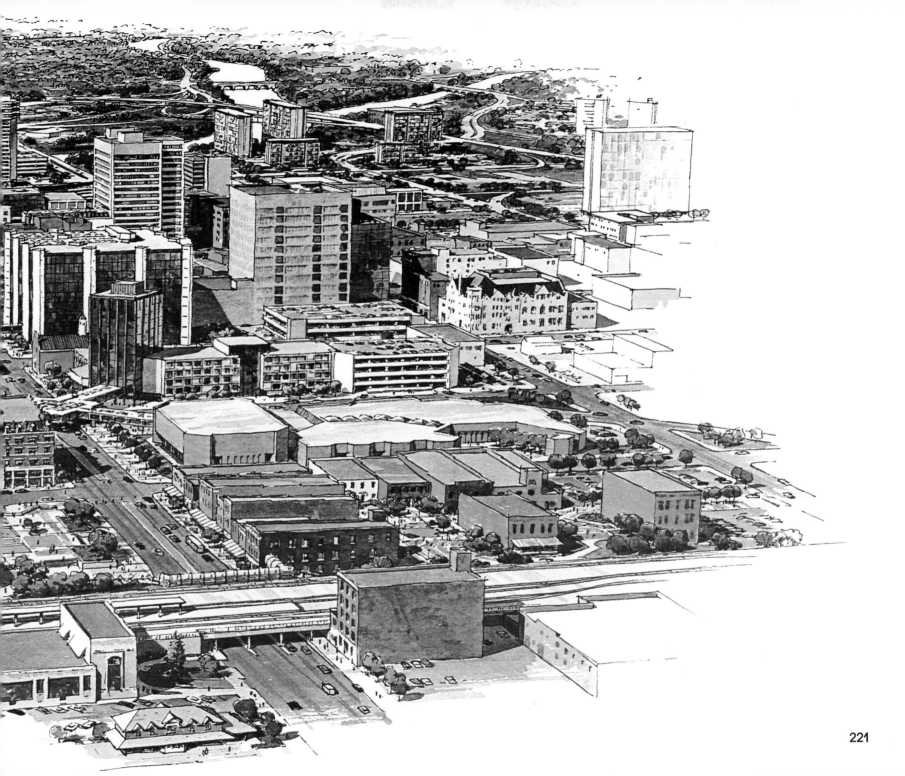

Doran Barham, illustrator, Wichita, KS. Watercolor on 16"-x-40" watercolor board. 55 hours.

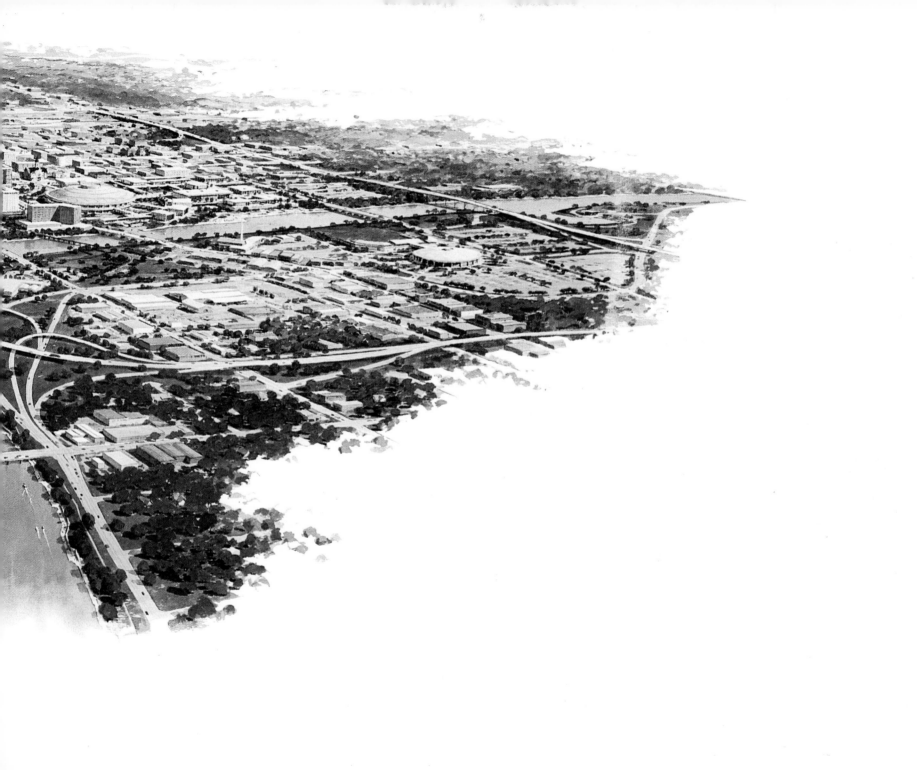

Dick Sneary, illustrator, Kansas City, MO. Watercolor on 30"-x-30" art-sepia print (original, pencil on vellum). 20 hours.

INTERIOR
ILLUSTRATIONS

6

Jim Hayes, illustrator, Honolulu, HI. Carbon pencil on 16"-x-26" vellum. 16 hours.

Craig Patterson, professor, University of Kansas. Ink on 11"-x-17" vellum. 24 hours.

Dick Sneary, illustrator, Kansas City, MO. Ink pen on 12"-x-16" vellum. 4 hours.

Dick Sneary, architect, Kansas City, MO. Colored pencil on 10"-x-14" vellum. 3 hours.

John Yancey, student, Kansas State University. Colored pencil on 10″-x-10″ yellow tracing paper. 5 hours.

Dick Sneary, architect, Kansas City, MO. *Left:* Pastel and colored pencil on 22"-x-31" yellow tracing paper. 10 hours. *Right:* Colored paper on 12"-x-16" vellum. 5 hours.

Dick Sneary, illustrator, Kansas City, MO. Pastel and colored pencil on 24"-x-24" vellum. 12 hours.

Dick Sneary, illustrator, Kansas City, MO. Pastel and colored pencil on 24"-x-30" photo-mural enlargement paper (original, pencil on 14"-x-18" vellum). 12 hours.

Dick Sneary, illustrator, Kansas City, MO. *Left*: Sharpie pen on 14"-x-19" marker paper. 1 hour. (T)
Right: Marker and colored pencil on 14"-x-19" vellum. 22 hours.

234

Craig Roberts, illustrator, Ft. Lauderdale, FL. Marker on 24"-x-30" rice paper. 6 hours.

Craig Roberts, illustrator, Ft. Lauderdale, FL. Marker on 24"-x-30" rice paper. 6 hours.

Dick Dee, landscape architect, Ft. Lauderdale, FL. Marker on 24"-x-36" black-line diazo print paper (original, felt-tip pen on vellum). 4 hours.

Robert Short, student, Kansas State University. Marker and felt-tip pen on 16"-x-22" white tracing paper. 4 hours.

Marshall Associates, Dallas, TX. *Top sheet:* Acrylic and marker painted on the back of line-printed acetate film. *Bottom sheet:* Marker on 11"-x-18" vellum. 10 hours total.

Watercolor on 12"-x-16" watercolor board. 5 hours each.

Carlos Diniz Associates, Los Angeles, CA. Acrylic on 26"-x-26" photo-mural paper (original, ink on vellum). 208 hours.

Recommended Rendering Materials

PENCILS
Pencils #2: HB, 2B, 6B; KOH-I-NOOR "Negro" No. 2; Wolff's Carbon BB, Eagle 314; Dixon No. 303; 6B Carpenter Pencil.

INKS
Rapidograph pen set (000—4); Sharpie by Sanford's; felt-tip pens by Flair, Pilot, Shaeffer.

COLORED PENCILS
Berol Prismacolor pencils: white, warm gray very light, warm gray light, black; blush, carmine red, scarlet red, crimson lake, orange; cream, canary yellow, yellowochre, raw umber, sepia, flesh; green bice, apple green, olive green, grass green, true green; nonphoto blue, true blue, copenhagen blue, indigo blue, aquamarine.

PASTELS
Eberhard Faber Nupastel; Grumbacher Golden palette pastels; 12 or 24 square stick.

WATERCOLORS
Brush no. 3, 8 round, 2" flat; frisket material; salt; pocket knife; dish; Winsor & Newton colors: Winsor Blue, Cobalt Blue, Cadmium Red, Cadmium Yellow, Alizarin Crimson, Ivory Black, Burnt Sienna, Raw Sienna, Burnt Umber, Sepia, Thalo Green, Hookers Green (medium).

TEMPERAS
Brush no. 3, 8 round; ¼", ⅜", 1", and 2" flat; tape; Pelikan graphic white; Winsor & Newton Watercolor Blue; Designers Gouache: Burnt Sienna, Burnt Umber, Jet Black, Grenadine, Permanent Green Deep, Golden Yellow, Lemon Yellow.

MARKERS

Color	Berol Marker	Design Marker	AD Marker
Gray	Warm #10%	Warm Gray #2	Warm Gray #1
	#30%	#4	#3
	#50%	#6	#5
	#70%	#8	#8
	Black	Black	Super Black
Red	Flesh	Light Flesh	Powder Pink
	Brick Red	Red Orange #1	Coral
	Cherry	Red #8	Life Red
	Dark Brick Red	Red #9	Maroon
		Red Orange	Cadmium Orange

Color	Berol Marker	Design Marker	AD Marker
Red Brown	Blush	Light Flesh	Sunset Pink
	Flagstone Red	Flesh	Peach
	Dark Brick Red	Pale Cherry	Burnt Sienna
		Red Brown	Burnt Umber
Brown	Brick Beige	Brown #0	Light Sand
	Sand	Raw Wood	Sand
	Burnt Ochre	Pale Walnut	Umber
	Walnut	Red Brown #9	Delta Brown
	Dark Brown		
Yellow Brown	Blonde Wood	Yellow #1	Naples Yellow
	Mustard	Yellow Orange #1	Gold
	Yellow Ochre	Yellow Orange	Yellow Ochre
	Bark	Yellow Brown	Kraft Brown
	Dark Brown	Yellow Brown #8	
Yellow Green	Cream	Yellow #1	Light Ivy
	Lime Green	Yellow Green Yellow	Medium Olive
	Spanish Olive	Green Orange Green	Dark Olive
	Marine Green	Green Orange Green #9	Slate Blue
Green	Willow Green	Green Yellow Green #1	Willow Green
	Grass Green	Green Yellow Green	Apple Green
	Dark Green	Green	Jade
		Green #9	Evergreen
			Nile Green
Blue	Nonphoto Blue	Blue #0	Sapphire Blue
	Light Blue	Blue #1	Blue Glow
	Process Blue	Blue Green Blue	Light Blue
	True Blue	Blue #9	Dutch Blue
	Copenhagen		Peacock Blue
Blue Green	Nonphoto Blue	Blue #0	Frost Blue
	Light Blue	Blue Green #1	Aquamarine
	Aquamarine	Blue Green	Sea Green
	Teal Blue	Blue Green #9	Blue Green

References

ENTOURAGE

Burden, Ernest. *Entourage: A Tracing File for Architecture and Interior Design Drawing*. New York: McGraw-Hill, 1981.

Szabo, Marc. *Drawing File for Architects, Illustrators, and Designers*. New York: Van Nostrand Reinhold, 1976.

PLAN, SECTION, ELEVATION

Walker, Theodore D. *Plan Graphics*. Mesa, Arizona: PDA Publishers Corporation, 1975.

Wang, Thomas C. *Plan and Section Drawing*. New York: Van Nostrand Reinhold, 1979.

RENDERING TECHNIQUES

Atkins, William. *Architectural Presentation Techniques*. New York: Van Nostrand Reinhold, 1976.

Calle, Paul. *The Pencil*. New York: Watson-Guptill, 1974.

Doyle, Michael E. *Color Drawing: A Marker-Colored-Pencil Approach*. New York: Van Nostrand Reinhold, 1981.

Dudley, Leavitt. *Architectural Illustration*. New York: McGraw-Hill, 1977.

Halse, Albert O. *Architectural Rendering: The Technique of Contemporary Presentation*. 2nd ed. New York: McGraw-Hill, 1972.

Kautzky, Ted. *The Ted Kautzky Pencil Book*. New York: Van Nostrand Reinhold, 1979.

————. *Ways with Watercolor*. 2nd ed. New York: Van Nostrand Reinhold, 1963.

Leach, Sid Delmar. *Techniques of Interior Design Rendering and Presentation*. New York: McGraw-Hill, 1978.

Lin, Mike W. *Architectural Presentation*. Taiwan: Ko-Chung Company, 1969.

Oles, Steve. *Architectural Illustration*. New York: Van Nostrand Reinhold, 1979.

Oliver, Robert. *Sketches in Color*. New York: Van Nostrand Reinhold, 1984.

Wang, Thomas C. *Pencil Sketching*. New York: Van Nostrand Reinhold, 1977.

————. *Sketching with Markers*. New York: Van Nostrand Reinhold, 1981.

RENDERING EXAMPLES

Burden, Ernest. *Architectural Delineation*. New York: McGraw-Hill, 1982.

Jacoby, Helmut. *New Architectural Drawings*. New York: Praeger, 1969.

Kemper, Alfred M. *Presentation Drawings by American Architects*. New York: John Wiley & Sons, 1977.

Walker, Theodore D. *Perspective Sketches*. 3rd ed. Mesa, Arizona: PDA Publishers Corporation, 1975.

Illustration Credits

Abend, Singleton Associates, Inc., Kansas City, MO: 91 (top)
Architectural Design Group, Ft. Lauderdale, FL: 162, 163, 235
Bacci Design, Boynton Beach, FL: 173
Badgett, Culver, Brandon, Oklahoma City, OK: 214, 215
Belt, Collins, and Associates, Honolulu, HI: 132, 133, 134, 168, 169, 170, 171, 226
Bertone and Farina Associates, Watchung, NJ: 81
BG Engineering, Manhattan, KS: 175
Rodger Brooks, Wichita, KS: 20, 213
Stuart Cohen, Miami, FL: 178, 179
Communication Arts, Boulder, CO: 157
Design Associates, Denver, CO: 207
Howard, Needles, Tammen, and Bergendoff, Kansas City, MO: 188, 189, 190, 191, 234
George Hunt and Associates, Dallas, TX: 12–19, 79
Johnson, Johnson, and Roy, Inc., Ann Arbor, MI: 78, 94, 128, 172
Kim Kiser and Nancy Steele, Wichita, KS: 239 (right)
Kwok Kong, Hong Kong: 205
Al Korsir, Bismark, ND: 206
LandDesign, Inc., Charlotte, NC: 75, 76, 77
Land Design/Research, Inc., Columbia, MD: 135, 136, 137
Clifford Landress, Miami, FL: 177
Phil Lawrence Associates, St. Joseph, MO: 232
Little Associates, Inc., Charlotte, NC: 212
Maguire Partners, Los Angeles, CA: 192, 193

Marshall and Brown, Kansas City, MO: 218
Marshall, Brown, and Sidorowicz, Kansas City, MO: 216, 217
Lee McCleskey Miller, Inc., Hilton Head, SC: 209
Nearing and Staats, Shawnee Mission, KS: 91 (bottom)
Nichols Partnership, Inc., Coral Gables, FL: 210, 211
PBNDML, Kansas City, MO: 181
Edward Pilkington, Miami, FL: 176, 177
Planning Development Services, Inc. (formerly Oblinger-Smith Corporation), Wichita, KS: 187, 202, 203, 204, 219, 220, 221, 222, 223
The Reimann, Buechner Partnership, Syracuse, NY: 74, 131
Robeson, Kuhnel, and Spangenberg, Wichita, KS: 186, 244
Seligson and Egan, Kansas City, MO: 143, 228
Shaughnessy, Fickel, and Scott, Kansas City, MO: 182
Siena Company, Boulder, CO: 157
Skidmore, Owings, Merrill, Chicago, IL: 195
Skidmore, Owings, Merrill, San Francisco, CA: 195
Skidmore, Owings, Merrill, Washington, D.C.: 194
Soloman, Claybaugh, Young, Kansas City, MO: 144
Edward D. Stone, Jr. and Associates, Ft. Lauderdale, FL: 72, 80, 161, 162, 163, 236, 237
Frederick Trough, Kansas City, MO: 151, 233
Harry Weese and Associates, Chicago, IL: 148
Wimberly, Whisenand, Allison, Tong, and Goo, Architects, Ltd., Honolulu, HI: 180
Thomas Zimmerman, Boulder, CO: 157

About the Author

Mike Lin is currently Professor of Landscape Architecture at Kansas State University, where he teaches both design and graphic-delineation courses. A registered landscape architect in the state of Kansas, his degrees include an undergraduate degree in architecture from Taiwan Institute of Technology, Taiwan, and a Master of Science in landscape architecture from the University of Wisconsin.

Recognized as one of the leaders in his field, Mike Lin has taught graphics and delineation classes for the last fifteen years. During this time he has given numerous graphic workshops and seminars at nearly forty-five universities and at many different cities across the United States. Because of the effectiveness of his teaching approach, he has been sponsored three times by the American Society of Landscape Architects to conduct one-day workshops across the country.

A member of the American Society of Landscape Architects, Mr. Lin has written one previous book, *Architectural Presentation.* In addition to teaching, he currently provides design and rendering services and gives graphic workshops twice a year at Kansas State University and to many organizations and universities throughout the United States.